Tarantulas

MICHAEL ANDREAS JACOBI

Tarantulas

Project Team
Editor: Thomas Mazorlig
Indexer: Sonja Armstrong
Design Concept: Leah Lococo Ltd.,
Stephanie Krautheim
Design Layout: Patricia Escabi

TFH Publications®
President/CEO: Glen S. Axelrod
Executive Vice President: Mark E. Johnson
Publisher: Christopher T. Reggio
Production Manager: Kathy Bontz

TFH Publications, Inc.®
One TFH Plaza
Third and Union Avenues
Neptune City, NJ 07753

Discovery Communications, LLC. Book Development Team: Marjorie Kaplan, President and General Manager, Animal Planet Media/ Kelly Day, Executive Vice President and General Manager, Discovery Commerce/ Elizabeth Bakacs, Vice President, Licensing and Creative/ JP Stoops, Director, Licensing/ Bridget Stoyko, Associate Art Director, Licensing

Printed and bound in China.
11 12 13 14 15   1 3 5 7 9 8 6 4 2

Library of Congress Cataloging-in-Publication Data
Jacobi, Michael Andreas.
  Tarantulas / Michael Andreas Jacobi.
    p. cm. – (Animal planet pet care library)
  Includes bibliographical references and index.
  ISBN 978-0-7938-3710-6 (alk. paper)
  1. Tarantulas as pets. I. Title.
  SF459.T37J33 2011
  639'.7–dc23
                              2011016696

The Leader in Responsible Animal Care for Over 50 Years!®
www.tfh.com

CENTRAL
Garden & Pet

Table of Contents

Chapter 1

The Tarantula

Allure

Big hairy spiders inspire awe in many people and fear in most. If a tiny spider in a dark kitchen corner is scary, a hairy arachnid with a leg span approaching the diameter of a dinner plate is downright fearsome. But appearances are deceptive. Powerful yet fragile and efficient yet primitive, tarantulas are more mysterious than scary. But there is no mystery to why these incredible spiders have become increasingly popular as terrarium pets. They require little space and minimal care. Most are inexpensive, as are the items required for proper care. They have fascinating habits and many are colorful, even beautiful, and some may live 25 years or more.

So, what are tarantulas and what makes them rewarding terrarium pets? Tarantulas are primitive spiders called mygalomorphs, a group that includes trapdoor and funnel-web spiders. Although they share their basic form with other spiders—a body divided into two segments with eight legs and two leg-like pedipalps attached to the front body segment (the prosoma)—their chelicerae, or fanged jaws, move vertically (forward and backward) not laterally (side to side), as is the case with other spiders. Tarantulas are efficient predators that ambush their prey instead of catching it in a silken web.

The 920 or so species of tarantula inhabit most of the warmer areas of the Earth. Some species have adapted to an arboreal lifestyle and are found among the bark and foliage of bushes and trees. Others are opportunistic terrestrial spiders that hunt and find shelter on the ground, occupying abandoned mammal burrows or hiding beneath leaf litter and rocks. But the majority of tarantulas are fossorial. That is, they are burrowers that tunnel into the earth and avoid predators and harsh weather in a snug chamber perhaps 2 feet (61 cm) below ground.

The largest tarantulas live in South America, where the Venezuelan species *Theraphosa apophysis* (known in the hobby as the Pink-Footed Goliath Bird-Eater) may reach a leg span of about 11 inches (27.9 cm). The "regular" Goliath Bird-Eater (*Theraphosa blondi*) has a slightly smaller leg span, but it has a heavier build. Large females of this species may weigh a quarter of a pound (113.4 g). However, there are plenty of small species among the world's tarantula fauna; for instance, the United States' native *Aphonopelma paloma*, an inhabitant of Arizona, has an adult leg span of about an inch (2.5 cm).

Tarantulaculture: Tarantulas as Pets

There are many reasons humans are drawn to keeping other animals. However, the husbandry of captive terrarium animals—those that offer

More than 100 species of tarantulas are now being bred for the pet trade, including beautiful and desirable species such as the Mexican Red-Knee.

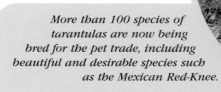

What's in a Name?

In America we refer to theraposid spiders (members of the family Theraphosidae) as tarantulas. This name originated in 14th Century southern Europe and did not even refer to theraposids, but rather the lycosids or wolf spiders and the widow spiders (*Latrodectus*). These two spiders were found in the Italian village of Taranto, and their venomous bites were said to cause a hypnotic hysteria termed tarantism in victims that did not die altogether.

But "tarantula" is not the only term used colloquially to describe theraposids. "Bird spider" is also very prevalent and is most often attributed to paintings by Madame Maria Merian, a German naturalist who in the late 1600s depicted her own encounters with a theraposid eating a bird. Other European travelers also brought home their tales of giant spiders that eat birds and other large prey. Today the term "bird eater" is most often used in the hobby for the giant *Theraphosa* (which live in deep burrows and likely eat few flighted animals) and a variety of, also ground-dwelling, Asian species.

The third most common popular term for theraposids is "baboon spider." This word is applied to many African species and is a reference to the resemblance of their furry legs to the fingers of baboons.

limited or no companionship yet otherwise bring pleasure to their human keepers—is a comparatively recent phenomenon. This pursuit—whether you prefer keeping reptiles, amphibians, aquarium fish, or tarantulas—brings a touch of nature into the home and provides a miniature window into the fascinating behavior of small exotic animals.

Tarantulas were housed in the London Zoo's insect house in the early 1900s, so we know that arachnid captive husbandry dates at least from that era. But it is only in the last 30 years or so that its popularity surged to the point that there is now a network of keepers,

many with an interest in captive breeding. After getting its spark in the early 1980s, the popular interest in keeping tarantulas has exploded in recent years. Although several people have laid claim to inventing the term *arachnoculture*, which refers to the captive care and breeding of arachnids, in truth it is just a natural adaptation of terms popularized most recently by captive reptile and amphibian husbandry and propagation (*herpetoculture*), and long before that by those who keep and breed birds (*aviculture*). With this book I have further adapted this nomenclatural progression in coining *tarantulaculture*.

With a leg span sometimes reaching over 10 inches (25 cm), the Brazilian Salmon-Pink Tarantula rivals the Goliath Bird-Eater in size but makes a better pet.

Tarantula Classification

All organisms are classified by biologists into groups that are further divided into a series of subgroups that contain increasingly related organisms. Like all other spiders and other arachnids, tarantulas are arthropods; that is, they belong to the phylum Arthropoda. This means that they are invertebrates (without a backbone) that have jointed bodies and limbs. Other arthropods include insects and crustaceans. Spiders are separated from other arthropods and are placed in the subphylum Chelicerata. This separation is based on their lack of antennae and other less easily observed differences. Other members of Chelicerata include horseshoe crabs, mites, and ticks.

Tarantulas and other spiders are then distinguished as arachnids (class Arachnida) along with scorpions, solifugids, whipscorpions, and others. The order Araneae is the spiders and the suborder Mygalomorphae includes tarantulas, trapdoor spiders, and the Australasian funnel-web spiders. The tarantulas are separated from other members of the Mygalomorphae (called mygalomorphs) into the family Theraphosidae, which is currently divided into eleven subfamilies. These subfamilies are then divided into genera (singular: genus) of very closely related species.

The genus and species give an organism its scientific name. This naming system is referred to as *binomial nomenclature*. Many people inaccurately use the term "Latin name" because these words are often derived from Latin, but they also have their origins in Greek and other languages, the names of people, and geography. *Etymology* refers to the meaning of words, and the etymology of many scientific names often gives clues to the organism's morphology (form and structure), color, and origin. For example, the scientific name of the tarantula hobby's most popular species, the Mexican Red-Knee (*Brachypelma smithi*), is composed of a genus name derived from Greek (*Brachy* = short, *pelma* = foot), and the species name refers to a person, H.H. Smith, who collected the original specimens. The name for the beautiful arboreal tarantula *Avicularia versicolor* comes from the Latin (*avicula* = small bird, *-aria* = pertaining to, *versicolor* = variegated, or changing colors).

Scientific names below the level of the family are always italicized (e.g. *Megaphobema mesomelas*); the genus name (in this case *Megaphobema*) is always capitalized, while the species name (*mesomelas*) always begins with a lower case letter. When referring to two or more species of the same genus, the genus is usually spelled out only the first time and then is abbreviated to the first initial in successive occurrences. For example, my three favorite species of tiger spiders or ornamental tarantulas are: *Poecilotheria subfusca*, *P. miranda*, and *P. ornata*.

Scientific names are much more accurate than common or vernacular names, and they give hobbyists a universal language. The fact is that common names are vague. A vernacular name like "Asian black" could refer to dozens of tarantulas. I use common names in this book only because they are still ubiquitous in American tarantulaculture—especially in the pet trade—but I do so with much hesitation. Because our hobby is truly global, the use of scientific names in Internet discussions is very important.

The Tarantula Body

The body of the tarantula is divided into two parts: the *prosoma* (or cephalothorax) and the *opisthosoma* (or

Example Tarantula Classification

Here is an example of the complete scientific classification of a tarantula. The Mexican Red-Knee Tarantula, a popular pet species, will serve as the example.

Phylum: Arthropoda
Subphylum: Chelicerata
Class: Arachnida
Order: Araneae
Suborder: Mygalomorphae
Family: Theraphosidae
Subfamily: Theraphosinae
Genus: *Brachypelma*
Species: *smithi*

Tarantulas differ from most other spiders by having fangs that move vertically instead of horizontally. The fangs of a King Baboon Tarantula shown here.

system (brain). The opisthosoma is surrounded by an elastic covering that allows for swelling from eating and drinking. It contains the primary organs of the circulatory, respiratory, digestive, and reproductive systems. Attached to the rear of the opisthosoma are two pairs of *spinnerets*.

The notable features of the carapace are the turret of small eyes and a central depression known as the *thoracic groove*. The latter provides the muscular attachment for the underlying sucking stomach that a tarantula uses to ingest its food. The tiny eyes of the ocular tubercle seem out of proportion to the rest of the body; they likely serve to do little more than distinguish light and dark.

Legs and Other Appendages

Starting at the front of a tarantula, the first pair of appendages attached to the prosoma are the chelicerae (singular: chelicera). They consist of a basal segment containing the venom gland and a curved fang. The two chelicerae move independently of each other and are raised when the tarantula strikes. As the fangs are thrust into prey, the spider injects venom. Venom serves to subdue prey as cheliceral (or cuticular) teeth located beneath the fangs begin to mash the meal as the chelicerae are moved. The resulting mass of masticated prey is called a *bolus*. Although the venom of some animals, like snakes, helps break down the body

abdomen). The two are joined by a small cylindrical *pedicel*. This body arrangement is shared by other arachnids, such as scorpions and solifugids, and is unlike the three segments of the typical insect body. Attached to the prosoma of spiders are eight legs; insects have only six legs.

The prosoma consists of the carapace, which is a hard dorsal surface that contains the *ocular tubercle,* where eight tiny eyes are clustered, and the sternum beneath. It also includes the *chelicerae*, fangs, and mouthparts, as well as the eight walking legs and two pedipalps (leg-like sensory appendages). The prosoma also contains the tarantula's central nervous

External Tarantula Anatomy

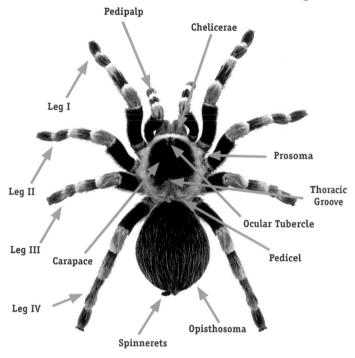

Pedipalp

Chelicerae

Leg I

Leg II

Leg III

Carapace

Leg IV

Spinnerets

Opisthosoma

Pedicel

Ocular Tubercle

Thoracic Groove

Prosoma

of prey, spider venom does not. Instead digestive juices from the tarantula's foregut are regurgitated through the mouth opening onto the bolus and then are sucked back into the foregut along with the liquefying meal. This is accomplished by means of a muscular sucking stomach.

On either side of the chelicerae is another pair of appendages called pedipalps. These six-segmented appendages look similar to the tarantula's four pairs of seven-segmented legs. When the tarantula is walking, the pedipalps function like an extra pair of legs but are used as feelers much like an insect uses antennae.

In mature (ultimate) males the last segment of the pedipalps is modified into a reproductive organ.

Four pairs of legs radiate from the soft junction of the prosoma's dorsum (carapace) and venter (sternum). Each leg has seven segments. From the body outward these segments are the *coxa, trochanter, femur, patella, tibia, metatarsus* and *tarsus*. (The six-segmented pedipalps lack the metatarsus). At the tip of the tarsus are two retractable tarsal claws. In some tarantulas, mature, or ultimate, males, have *tibial apophyses* (singular: *apophysis*). These are popularly referred to as mating spurs or hooks, and they engage with the female's fangs during mating. The individual legs on each side of the body are named using roman numerals. Leg I is to the front, followed by Leg II, Leg III and Leg IV as you move toward the rear. For example, to determine a tarantula's leg span you measure diagonally across the body, from the tip of Leg I on one side to the tip of Leg IV on the opposite side of the tarantula.

Some species of tarantula can produce a sound similar to hissing by rubbing two body surfaces called *stridulatory organs* together. These bristles and spines are found on the chelicerae and/or coxa, and the trochanter of the pedipalps and/or the first pair of legs. Stridulation is particularly well developed in the King Baboon Tarantula (*Pelinobius muticus*).

On the Bottom

Located on the underside of the opisthosoma are the openings for the respiratory and reproductive organs. Toward the anterior or front end of this ventral surface is a curved groove called the *epigastric furrow*. In the center of this suture is the opening for the sexual organs. In females the *epigynum,* or external genitalia, lies here and connects inside with sperm-storing receptacles called *spermathecae*. In males this opening is used to discharge sperm; just anterior to the opening are silk-producing organs called *epiandrous fusillae*. On either side of the epigastric furrow are two pairs of lung slits or *spiracles*, which are the openings of the *book lungs* a tarantula uses for respiration. These organs get their name from the fact that the numerous stacked surfaces, or lamellae, that function in gas exchange resemble the pages of a book.

Spinnerets

At the posterior of the opisthosoma are two pairs of flexible, finger-like appendages called *spinnerets*. The spider spins silk from these appendages. The anterior (or forward) pair is smaller and somewhat hidden by the much larger posterior (or rear) pair. These organs may be manipulated independently or in concert,

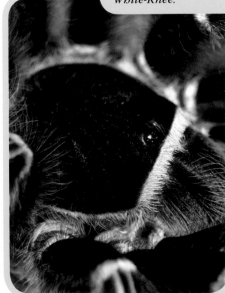

Tarantulas have eight small eyes grouped together on the ocular tubercle, shown here on a Brazilian Giant White-Knee.

Are Tarantulas Venomous?

One of the most common questions asked about tarantulas is whether they are venomous. The fact is that, yes, tarantulas are venomous, but their venom is mild and of little danger to a healthy human. People with allergies to bee venom and such would do best to avoid the possibility of a tarantula bite, but there are no documented cases of human fatality from tarantula envenomation. Like other spiders, tarantulas are not aggressive. They are defensive animals that would prefer fleeing but will defend themselves if bothered. A tarantula bite can be painful (after all, they have fairly large fangs and their venom) while not dangerous, a tarantula bite can produce a range of effects including pain and local swelling, muscular cramps, and, in a few rare cases, serious illness.

The truth is that tarantula venom has not been thoroughly studied, so we are unsure about its deleterious effects. However, researchers have begun to find positive applications for tarantula venom in medicine, including potential treatments of heart arrhythmia, Alzheimer's disease, and Parkinson's disease.

as the tarantula excretes silk from openings at their tips. The liquid silk solidifies as it is released and is produced from a number of glands that create different silk for different purposes.

Although tarantulas do not build prey-catching webs, they do use silk for other purposes such as leaving a trailing guideline; wrapping up a prey bolus during feeding; sealing the entrances of their burrows for protection from pests, predators, and the elements; and, in some species, creating a retreat. Females create a special silk to encase their egg sacs. Mature males use silk from both the spinnerets and epiandrous fusillae to create *sperm webs*.

Setae

The surface of the opisthosoma is covered by a dense coating of *setae*, or hairs. In many tarantulas from the New World there is a patch of *urticating hairs* on top of the opisthosoma that are used in defense. When the tarantula is disturbed it brushes these hairs off using its hind legs, and they serve as an itchy irritant to discourage further molestation by pests and predators. Humans vary in their sensitivity to these hairs, but immediate itching is often the result of contact. They are particularly irritating to the eyes and mucous membranes of the nose and mouth. In one genus, *Ephebopus*, the urticating hairs are found on the pedipalps, not the opisthosoma. It should be noted here that an oral antihistamine often provides relief for keepers that have a reaction to urticating hairs, and anti-itch antihistamine sprays can work wonders if applied to affected skin immediately after exposure.

The bristles that cover the tarantula's body are primary sensory structures. The bristles of the legs are particularly well developed, and most of tarantula bristles connect to the nervous system. Tarantulas have poor vision and cannot hear or smell (they do, however, perceive chemicals like pheromones), but they have an extremely responsive sense of touch. Any vibration, airborne or through contact, is processed by the tarantula's brain. This tactile perception of its world is one of the many fascinating aspects of tarantula biology.

Internal Anatomy

Inside the opisthosoma lie the tarantula's heart and its open circulatory system. In spiders, *hemolymph* serves as blood to carry oxygen and carbon dioxide. It is a milky white fluid with a faintly blue color. While most of the tarantula's body is encased in a hard exoskeleton, the opisthosoma's elastic covering allows it to balloon or shrink depending on nourishment and hydration.

Molting

Animals that are encased in a hard protective exoskeleton must shed this skin in order to grow. This process is called *ecdysis, or molting*. A tarantula's opisthosoma may swell and shrink based upon its water and food intake, but the rest of its body does not change in size between molts. Because molting an exoskeleton without having an immediate replacement would leave a spider without structural form, a new one begins forming beneath the old skin. It is slightly larger, wrinkled, and pliable, and a newly shed tarantula is soft and vulnerable. Over the next few days (or more) the tarantula will often rest in a stretched position, expanding the new exoskeleton as it hardens. It is during this time that the tarantula grows.

To find out how molting affects the care of your tarantula, see the section on it in chapter 2.

Developmental Stages

Arthropod development goes through stages called *stadia* (singular: stadium) that are separated by shedding the exoskeleton (ecdysis). *Instar* is another term for a stadium and is actually the more frequently used term.

Like other spiders, tarantulas create silk for webs with their spinnerets.

Instars

A tarantula begins life as an embryo—a fertilized egg. Inside the egg sac it develops and becomes a postembryo. European tarantula keepers refer to the postembryo as nymph-1. When the postembryo molts it becomes a motile nymph called a 1st instar (one molt). Normally tarantulas do not feed when they are postembryos or 1st instars, but many tarantula breeders have witnessed some degree of 1st instar cannibalization. Once again, Europeans use an alternative term, referring to 1st instars as nymph-2. American keepers do not use the terms nymph-1 and nymph-2, but may casually refer to either postembryos or 1st instars as nymphs.

When a 1st instar molts again it becomes a 2nd instar, which in most species is a fully pigmented, fully motile, feeding mini-tarantula. Every time the spider molts (successive stadia), it is considered the next highest instar, so it goes from 3rd instar to 4th instar and so on. Technically, if you raised it from a spiderling and counted each molt you might refer to your adult *Brachypelma smithi* as a 27th instar, even if that would be a bit silly.

Spiderling and Other Casual Terms

Tarantula keepers use the term *spiderling* (or *sling* or *s'ling*) to describe baby tarantulas. No matter how you write it, sling is part of the hobby vernacular and its use is widespread.

*Top: Many of the tarantulas from the western hemisphere defend themselves by kicking off the irritating hairs located on the abdomen. **Bottom:** Over time, these tarantulas may develop bald spots from kicking off the hairs.*

Spiderling is synonymous with the correct term *early instar*. One question new keepers often ask is at what age a spiderling becomes a juvenile. Since spiderling is not a technical term it can be hard to define. Arbitrary terms such as spiderling, juvenile, subadult, and adult are approximations, reflecting tarantula species differences in growth rates and life spans. An 8th instar Brazilian Black (*Grammostola pulchra*) is certainly still a young spider, while a 8th instar male Usambara Orange

Baboon (*Pterinochilus murinus*) may be mature. Personally, I call young tarantulas "spiderlings" until they are about 2 inches (5 cm) in diagonal leg span, but this certainly wouldn't work for a diminutive species like the Trinidad Dwarf (*Cyriocosmus elegans*), which never reaches this size. But for most tarantulas the 2-inch (5-cm) mark is my arbitrary cut-off, after which they are "juveniles" until they are approaching maturity and can be referred to as *preultimate*, *penultimate*, or *ultimate*.

Maturity

Male tarantulas change radically when they mature. The ends of their pedipalps become sexual organs. In many tarantulas, mating hooks are found on the underside of the first pair of legs. The male tarantula goes through its entire life without these organs, and then they appear with what is called his *ultimate molt*. Ultimate as in terminal, as most male tarantulas will never molt again. This is their final stage of life. So, in the case of males, ultimate is the stage (or stadium) of maturity. Males cannot breed prior to this stage. A male that has reached the size and age where its next molt will be ultimate is penultimate, or one before ultimate. Prior to that they are preultimate, and this term is often applied to any "subadult" or "adult" male that is not mature and it is unclear whether he will mature with his next molt and should be called penultimate. Females do not have a true ultimate molt, as they will continue to molt once

sexually mature. For females, using the vague terms subadult or adult is satisfactory.

Telling Males from Females

In most tarantulas the female and male look almost identical throughout most of their lives. That is until a male reaches maturity where he may look drastically different from the way he did prior to his maturing molt. Since females live much longer than males, they are more desirable to the pet keeper. However, telling the two sexes apart can be very difficult, especially for the novice keeper. People soon learn to recognize the characteristics of a mature male, but it can be much harder to distinguish between an immature male and a female, especially in young tarantulas.

The Mature Male

When a male has his ultimate molt and reaches sexual maturity he is a completely different spider. During this ultimate molting process he obtains his sexual organs, which are bulbs, or *emboli* (singular: *embolus*) on the end of his pedipalps that are used to transfer sperm from his sperm web to the female. The slang term for these palpal bulbs is boxing gloves—and they certainly give that appearance. In many species males also have tibial spurs, which are the so-called mating hooks on the underside of the tibia (or long segment) of the first pair of walking legs (Leg I) and are used to engage the female's fangs during mating. These two structures, the *tibial apophysis* (or spur) and the *embolus* (or palpal bulb) are the things to look for to determine whether you have a mature male. In some species the transformation is even more obvious, as mature males have distinctly different colors and patterns. In most tarantula species the males are much smaller and more

thinly built and "leggy" than females.

Although mature males may be obvious once you learn the characteristics, they often look very similar to the female prior to the ultimate molt. It is true that adult females are generally larger (often significantly so) and more heavily built than males, and that their chelicerae are proportionately broader. However these are subtle differences that only keepers with considerable experience and access to several specimens for comparison can rely on. They can fool even the experienced keeper. In some species, the coloration and pattern of subadult and adult females is different from that of males. For example, many ornamental tarantulas (*Poecilotheria* species) can be visually sexed prior to maturity by the foliate pattern on the abdomen. This also requires experience and comparison, but it does make these species easier to sex.

These are 1st instar Brazilian Salmon-Pink Tarantulas. In most species, the spiderlings do not eat until reaching the 2nd instar.

FAMILY-FRIENDLY TIP

Is a Tarantula a Good Pet for a Child

A tarantula can be an excellent first pet for the conscientious child, because tarantulas are fairly easy to keep. Having the duties of providing one with food and water will help teach responsibility and offer an introduction to caring for another creature. And since a weekly feeding regimen and checking the water twice a week is adequate, tarantulas don't even require the daily attention of a goldfish, much less the frequent upkeep of other popular first pets like small mammals.

However, adult supervision is necessary at all times. Even the most docile tarantula species can deliver a painful bite or discomfort through its defensive urticating hairs. Also, tarantulas are extremely fragile creatures that can be fatally wounded by even a slight fall or impact from a fallen object. Tarantula care should be a joint experience shared by parent and child.

Microscopic Examination of Molts

The most accurate method of determining the sex of a live tarantula is to examine the interior of the abdominal portion of its *exuvium* (molted skin). A female tarantula sheds the spermathecae lining along with the rest of her exoskeleton, and an experienced examiner can look for the presence of the spermatheca, which are the sperm storage receptacles of the female. This usually requires the use of a stereo dissecting microscope with lighting above and below the stage, but spermathecae are visible to the naked eye on the exuvia of most large adult tarantulas.

Examining exuvia (molts) for the presence or absence of spermathecae requires experience, not only to recognize the spermathecae and distinguish it from male accessory organs but also in the laborious process of softening the skin and carefully unfolding the abdominal skin so that the four book lungs and the genital opening are stretched flat. It is very difficult to use a molt from a tarantula less than 2 inches (5 cm) in leg span, because it is often nearly impossible to unravel the twisted abdominal skin.

Because accurate sexing by this method requires a great deal of experience and a good microscope, it is best for most tarantula keepers to save their molts and send them to someone who will examine them at no cost. The Resources section in the back of this book lists some places, including that of the author, you can send a skin to for free tarantula sexing.

Longevity and Life Span

There are tarantulas that reach maturity quickly and have a short life span, and those that are slower to develop but may live 25 years or more. Females live considerably longer than males, which reach the end of their life cycle with their maturing, ultimate molt. Much of what we know about tarantula longevity is based upon tarantulas raised in captivity, where artificial conditions may affect development and life span. Food is plentiful for the tarantula in the terrarium, and dangers are almost nonexistent. For example, with frequent feeding and warm temperatures male Usambara Orange Tarantulas (*Pterinochilus murinus*) may have their ultimate molt less than 12 months after hatching. Breeders of arboreal tarantulas usually see male *Poecilotheria, Psalmopoeus*, and *Avicularia* species mature when they are 16 to 24 months old, with some maturing even earlier than that. In these tarantulas in captivity, females typically live five to eight years, with exceptional specimens living ten or twelve.

The longest-lived tarantulas appear to be those that inhabit grasslands and scrub desert. In these habitats, climate changes throughout the year and periods of growth are followed by periods of dormancy. These species—including many of the tarantula hobby's most popular and suitable pets, such as members of the genera *Brachypelma* and *Grammostola*—may take five to eight years to reach maturity, and their life spans can exceed 30 years.

Epiandrous Fusillae Method

Male tarantulas, even those who have yet to reach their ultimate molt, have additional spinnerets (*fusillae*) just anterior to the center of the *epigastric furrow* that are connected to silk-producing *epiandrous* glands. The fusillae appear as a darker triangular or semi-circular shape. These auxiliary organs are used in sperm web production. The presence (indicating a male) or absence (indicating a female) of these fusillae is a reliable indicator of sex. Although it can be difficult to use this method reliably in young tarantulas, with good light and a keen eye many keepers can sex their subadults and adults using this method.

Chapter 2

Your Pet

Tarantula

So you are considering a tarantula pet, right? Welcome to the legions of spider enthusiasts who find these big hairy creatures fascinating. Tarantulas are such excellent terrarium subjects that most keepers quickly become engrossed in tarantulaculture. The more you learn about the animal, the more you'll want to learn about its world. Perhaps you already have a tarantula and want to ensure that it receives the best possible care. Kudos to you and your commitment to responsible pet ownership.

Tarantulas are pretty undemanding, but there are plenty of considerations to be aware of—like diet, housing, and environment. When you learn everything you can about your tarantula, you create a win-win situation: Your pet is happy and healthy and you derive the greatest enjoyment from the hobby. In this chapter you will learn a great deal about the exciting world of tarantulas in the terrarium.

Choosing a Tarantula

One of the questions most frequently asked is "which tarantula is best for the beginner?" Certainly each keeper's needs are different, but typically what a person seeks in his or her first tarantula is one that is easy to care for and calm in temperament. Generally speaking, tarantulas are low-maintenance pets, but those that are easiest to care for are those that can be maintained at room temperature in a warm home without any supplemental heat and also tolerate a dry cage with a small water dish supplying the only moisture. These are the grassland or desert species. Tropical varieties may require a little more warmth and almost always require somewhat elevated humidity.

As for temperament, beginning keepers also understandably desire a species that is not likely to bite. Some keepers wish to hold their tarantulas. This is a controversial subject that is addressed later in this book. But many of the species listed on pages 24 and 25 are those that have dispositions that lend themselves to handling if the keeper chooses. Not surprisingly, these species are all from the Americas and are therefore known as New World tarantulas. The Old World tarantulas—those from Africa and Asia—are best left to more experienced keepers, as they generally have much more defensive temperaments.

Buying a Tarantula

There are many reasons why captive-bred animals are superior, not the least of which are health and longevity and not contributing to the capture of wild animals and destruction of habitat. Buying young captive-bred tarantulas allows you to raise them and watch them grow for many years.

The number of tarantula species that is now available is large to the point of being daunting. It can be difficult to decide which one is right for you. Many rare types are now captive-bred and are becoming more and more affordable. When you learn more about tarantulas and decide which species you want to buy, you can begin canvassing your local pet shops, especially those that specialize in reptiles and other non-mammalian pets. You will begin to see what is available and at what price, and you can begin shopping for the supplies you will need to create a suitable terrarium.

Although there are advantages to purchasing a tarantula in person, such as being able to assess its health, age, and species, it may be difficult to locate your desired species in your area. More and more pet stores are carrying young captive-bred tarantulas, but finding a

The Chilean Rose-Hair is a common and inexpensive tarantula, but its often poor appetite can make it frustrating to keep.

spiderling of your chosen species locally may still be challenging.

As you continue your research into tarantulas and their care, you will discover that there are quite a few fellow tarantulaculturists—including professional tarantula dealers—selling and trading spiders. Exchanging animals with fellow hobbyists will establish new friendships and create networking opportunities for breeding loans and trades down the line, but it is the expertise of the long-term tarantula dealer/breeder that will be most beneficial to you. Check classified advertisements on popular web forums (see the Resources section in the back of this book) and read dealer reviews posted by members of these sites. You will soon discover who the most reputable dealers are, and forging a relationship with these tarantula sellers will benefit you greatly. Tarantula dealers are well versed in safely packaging tarantulas and shipping them via overnight delivery services to your doorstep, and most have a live arrival guarantee. Hundreds of species are available this way, almost definitely including the species you decide to keep.

Housing

Tarantulas should be housed in small enclosures that are safe and secure. Owners must exercise care to ensure that the enclosure is protected from other pets, such as dogs and cats, and

Ground-Dwelling Species

Scientific Name	Common Name	Comments
Aphonopelma seemanni	Stripe-Knee or Costa Rican Zebra	The wide-ranging genus *Aphonopelma* includes the spiders of the American Southwest, which are plainly colored but hardy and easy to keep. The most popular member of the genus is a much more attractive Central American species known as the Stripe-Knee.
Brachypelma albopilosum	Central American or Honduran Curly-Hair	This Central American tarantula has long woolly golden-brown hairs and is large and gentle. It is fairly inexpensive and easy to raise, making it a terrific first tarantula.
Brachypelma smithi	Mexican Red-Knee	This has been the most popular pet tarantula for many years, and despite its penchant for flicking urticating hairs, it remains an exceptional choice for a first tarantula.
Brachypelma boehmei *Brachypelma emilia* *Brachypelma auratum*	Mexican Fire-Leg Mexican Painted Red-Leg Mexican Flame-Knee	These three tarantulas and several others are essentially just differently colored and patterned versions of the more well-known *B. smithi*. Captive care and behavior is identical for all of the red-legs.
Chromatopelma cyaneopubescens	Greenbottle Blue	This outrageously colorful tarantula is a bit more nervous than the others in this list, but it is unlikely to bite and makes a gorgeous display spider. It is also extremely easy to raise and keep.
Eupalaestrus campestratus	Pink Zebra Beauty	This amazingly docile and attractive species used to be abundant in the pet trade, but since wild-caught imports from Paraguay have ceased, it is much more difficult to find.

Grammostola porteri (formerly known as *G. rosea*)	Chilean Rose-Hair or Chilean Rose	This is the most common tarantula in the pet trade, with a seemingly endless supply of wild-caught adults making their way into pet shops. However, this is a problematic species (see Chapter 6) that frustrates many new keepers and may discourage further exploration of the tarantula hobby.
Grammostola pulchra	Brazilian Black	I refer to this spider as the "Black Labrador Retriever" of the tarantula world. It is big, black, and very docile. A better pet spider cannot be found.
Grammostola pulchripes (formerly know as *G. aureostriata*)	Chaco Gold-Striped or Chaco Gold-Knee	If the Brazilian Black is the "black lab," the Chaco Gold is certainly the "Golden Retriever." This is a hardy and beautiful tarantula with a very gentle disposition.

Tree-Dwelling Species

Scienific Name	Common Name	Comments
Avicularia versicolor *Avicularia metallica*	Antilles Pink-Toe Metallic White-Toe or Metallic Pink-Toe	The Common Pink-Toe (*Avicularia avicularia*) is readily available in the form of wild-caught adults found in pet stores. However, captive bred spiders are much more desirable, and these two species are good choices among the dozen or more species of *Avicularia* available. *A. versicolor* is an incredibly beautiful spider, and *A. metallica* is one of the larger and most docile members of the genus.

placed out of reach of children. Locate it in an area out of direct sunlight or drafts and where there is little disturbance from vibration such as heavy foot traffic and loud music.

Enclosure Size

New keepers often use enclosures that are too large. Tarantulas naturally live in burrows, tree holes, or other small confined places and need the security of a small space. A small cage also allows you to easily monitor feeding and promptly remove uneaten food or prey remains. As a rule of thumb, an enclosure should be two or three times the leg span of the tarantula in both width and length (and height in the case of arboreal species). It is also highly recommended that the distance from the top of the substrate to the top of the cage be no more than the tarantula's leg span for terrestrial (ground-dwelling) species. This is to prevent injury from a fall. In the unnatural situation of captivity, some heavy-bodied tarantulas that would normally not climb in the wild will scale the sides of an aquarium and explore

the tops of their cages. This can be a dangerous situation, but it can easily be avoided by using shorter, low-profile enclosures or reducing the distance from the surface to the top with deep substrate.

Types of Enclosures

You can keep your adult tarantula in a very simple and inexpensive plastic container with numerous air holes in the sides and lid or a more expensive glass or acrylic terrarium with a screen lid (see the section: Raising Young Tarantulas for suitable housing

The Expert Knows

Safe Environment

Tarantulas are very sensitive to toxins, so you must be sure your pet's environment is free of harmful chemicals. Many common household products can injure or kill a tarantula. Nicotine is a powerful insecticide, and it's best to keep tobacco smoke away from tarantulas. (While tarantulas aren't insects, most insecticides will kill them just the same.) Cleaning products, overheated nonstick cookware, and other household items may also release noxious fumes. Use caution when cleaning or disinfecting a tarantula's enclosure; be sure that you rinse it thoroughly after cleaning and that fumes such as those from chlorine bleach have dissipated. Of course, any type of insecticide or natural bug deterrent like neem oil must be kept far away from your tarantula. Your pet deserves a safe, clean, comfortable place to live.

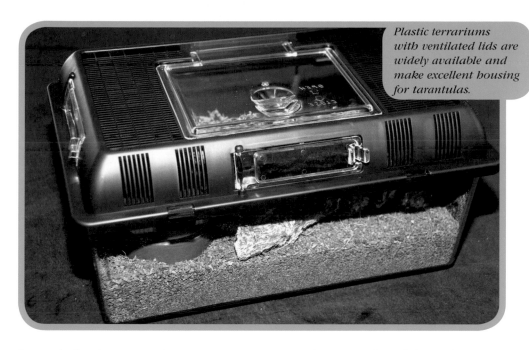

Plastic terrariums with ventilated lids are widely available and make excellent housing for tarantulas.

for spiderlings). Various clear storage containers and craft displays can also make excellent tarantula enclosures with the addition of holes or screening for ventilation.

Perhaps the most popular tarantula cage is the plastic terrarium or critter keeper, and this type of housing is exceptionally good for many types of tarantula. These small terrariums have a snap-on well-ventilated lid with an access door. They can be found at most pet stores, and there are some new models that are shorter in height and excellent for terrestrial tarantulas. These low-profile models are marketed with names like "lizard lounge" or "breeder box" and are my recommendation for housing many popular pet tarantulas. Newer models include a sliding side door so that the keeper can insert food

even when a number of these plastic terrariums are stacked.

Clear plastic storage containers, which are sold as shoe boxes, sweater boxes, etc., are very popular with keepers housing large numbers of tarantulas. They don't make for very attractive displays, but with the addition of ventilation in the sides and top they make very functional tarantula enclosures. They are particularly well-suited to housing large tropical tarantulas like the Goliath Bird-Eater (*Theraphosa blondi*) and Colombian Lesser Black (*Xenesthis immanis*). Breeders of these types of tarantulas use 66-quart (62.5-l) or larger tubs and fill them with a foot or more of substrate to facilitate large deep burrows. Similarly, tall clear containers such as those used for cereal storage

The Basic Tarantula Terrarium

For popular pet tarantulas like the Chilean Rose-Hair (*Grammostola porteri*) and Mexican Fire-Leg (*Brachypelma boehmei*), acquiring the basic supplies to create a suitable enclosure is easy.

The following items are available at pet superstores and smaller pet shops that sell reptiles:

- Enclosure: Low-profile plastic terrarium
- Substrate: Coconut coir (also called coconut husk bedding)
- Hiding Place: Coconut shell hide
- Water Dish: Small shallow bowl
- Temperature and Humidity Gauge: Small digital meter

If supplemental heat becomes necessary add:

- Heat Mat: Mini under-tank heat mat (Note: Place underneath one end of terrarium to create heat gradient and allow air space between heater and terrarium to prevent overheating. For safety and temperature control regulate with a thermostat).

are used by many breeders to house either arboreal tarantulas or smaller burrowing tarantulas that require deep substrate, like the Cobalt Blue (*Haplopelma lividum*).

Substrate

Substrate is the covering that goes on the bottom of the enclosure. It is sometimes called bedding, although tarantulas don't use it as such. The substrate gives your spider better traction than does the smooth plastic terrarium floor. Substrates may also provide burrowing opportunities and help regulate or maintain humidity.

Soils

Any sort of clean and natural soil that is free of pesticides and fertilizers is a good choice for a tarantula substrate. Chemical-free top or potting soil, peat moss, and coconut coir (popular as a reptile substrate and sold in compressed form) are excellent tarantula substrates. Horticultural vermiculite can also be used with great success, as it is inert and unlikely to harbor mold or fungi, but it is unnatural in appearance and dusty. There have been concerns about the presence of asbestos in some vermiculite products, but these products have been removed from the market. Do not use sand (except as a small part of a mixture containing mostly soil or peat), gravel, perlite, corn cob, or any other type of small animal bedding, especially cedar shavings.

The substrate should be as deep as the container allows, at least 2 inches (5

A Stripe-Knee outside its burrow in Costa Rica. In nature, tarantulas rarely stray far from their burrows.

cm) whenever possible. This will allow you to pour some water down the side and have the bottom depth damp while the surface in contact with the spider is dry. Ideally, it is good to have one slightly damp corner where the water dish is situated and have the opposite areas be dry. Over time this water will evaporate and provide beneficial humidity. Replenish as needed, taking care to not saturate the substrate.

My personal favorite substrate is a 50/25/25 percent mix of coconut coir, peat moss, and vermiculite respectively. There are terrarium mixes available that are similar, but using any sort of clean, chemical-free earth is absolutely fine. If you choose to use yard soil or other substrate collected outdoors, you may want to heat it in an oven at about 200°F (93°C) for an hour to kill tiny organisms, bacteria, mold, and fungus.

Mosses

In addition to the substrate, several mosses found in garden shops are useful in the tarantula terrarium. Sphagnum moss (not to be confused with peat moss that makes an excellent primary substrate) is very popular for its moisture retention. It is sometimes sold as "orchid moss" in plant and garden stores. A damp layer of sphagnum moss is often placed on top of the substrate to provide additional moisture and help prevent the soil below from drying too quickly. It is especially useful in containers used to raise spiderling tarantulas, and strands of it can be placed vertically to provide climbing surfaces for arboreal species.

Dried green moss can be found in garden and craft shops and is excellent for creating attractive displays. Live green moss can be obtained from

Review of Substrate Choices

MAY BE USED	PROS	CONS
Backyard soil	Cheap and easy to obtain.	May harbor predators, pests, mold, and fungus.
Coconut coir	Compressed bricks readily available in the pet trade. Excellent substrate that is environment-friendly (waste by-product of coconut industry).	May have a tendency to mold. Mostly sold in compressed bricks that have to be soaked to expand.
Peat moss	Acidity repels mold. Holds water well.	Often contains fungus spores. Mined from peat bogs, damaging an important ecological habitat.
Potting soil	Organic pestcide & fertilizer-free potting soils are attractive and functional. Best mixed with vermiculite.	May drain poorly unless mixed with vermiculite. Many products contain chemicals.
Vermiculite	Inexpensive, holds moisture well yet allows for drainage.	Unattractive and dusty.
Combination of the above	Many keepers have their own recipes for mixing two or more of the above, perhaps with a small percentage of sand added to aid drainage and improve structural integrity of burrows.	

NOT IN USE	REASON
Sand	Highly abrasive and may clog book lungs, mouthparts, etc., especially when wet. A small amount of sand can be added to terratium soil but should never be used alone.
Gravel	Abrasive, heavy, hard to clean—there really is nothing good about using gravel for anything other than as a drainage layer at the very bottom of a naturalistic terrarium.
Wood shavings	Cedar and many other woods contain oils that are toxic to invertebrate. Even those without these aromatic toxins, like aspen and pine, are of no use in tarantula care.
Corn cob	Corn cob small animal beddings absorb all of the moisture in air and are therefore terrible substrates for tarantulas (or reptiles and other terrarium pets).

tropical plant dealers and is fantastic for those who wish to create naturalistic terrariums for their tarantulas. It can be placed upon a layer of moist orchid moss to provide a rooting surface that will help it flourish in the terrarium. As with any live plants, the use of live moss in a tarantula terrarium will necessitate good lighting.

A 10-gallon (38-l) aquarium turned on its end works well for housing arboreal tarantulas, as seen in this breeder's colony.

Cage Décor

Tarantulas do not require plants or decorations, but you can use such items to make your pet's home more attractive. You can add plants, bark, hollow logs, or other items that fit your desires and your tarantula's habitat.

Plants

Silk or plastic plants are much more durable than live plants, and they eliminate the possibility of the substrate and cage becoming too wet from watering. Of course, fake plants also do not require light, and tarantulas prefer dark cages. Naturalistic terrariums with live plants are beautiful ways to showcase your tarantula, but only diffuse fluorescent light should be used and the terrarium should be illuminated for no more than ten hours a day to minimize light stress to the tarantula. If you use live plants, avoid those with spines or other sharp features.

Retreats and Other Decorations

Cork bark pieces, hollow logs, grapewood vine and driftwood are attractive items to decorate with. Most of these items are available at pet stores that sell reptiles and their supplies. Halved hollow logs and hide boxes made from hollow coconut shells provide your tarantula with a welcome retreat that is natural and attractive. Avoid any items that have sharp edges or are excessively rough in texture. Also avoid any decor from outdoors that may harbor pests or carnivorous insects, or that may have been exposed to pesticides, fertilizers, or other hazardous materials. When

31

The Naturalistic Terrarium

Most tarantulas thrive when housed in simple setups as described in this chapter. A basic enclosure with nothing more than substrate, a retreat, and a water dish—plus supplemental heat if required—is easy to maintain, and this contributes to the wellness of pet tarantulas.

However, many keepers wish to bring a touch of nature into their home and create a display that rivals the beauty of a well-planted dart frog terrarium or a saltwater aquarium. For those who are ready for the challenge of creating a miniature indoor rendering of a tropical rainforest or perhaps a desert scrubland, tarantulas can be suitable inhabitants.

Creators of naturalistic terrariums find themselves immersed in a hobby-within-a-hobby, as more time becomes devoted to the care of plants than the tarantula that lives among them. Some keepers use isopods and tropical woodlice as living soil cleaners; this adds yet another life form to the mix and further increases the enjoyment derived from keeping tarantulas in the terrarium.

While the creation of naturalistic terrariums is beyond the scope of this book, there are some good sources of information in the Resources section. Additionally you can find plenty of information on the Internet.

Arboreal tarantulas, such as Avicularia metallica, *can do very well and even breed in naturalistic terrariums.*

designing your enclosure, remember that terrestrial tarantulas like more ground space and a deeper substrate, whereas arboreal tarantulas need taller enclosures that are equipped with wood or plants they can climb and, in some cases, attach their silk nests to.

Drinking Water

Although tarantulas acquire most of their water from their food, it is a good idea to provide a small shallow dish of fresh water to adult tarantulas. The natural evaporation will also provide beneficial humidity. It is more difficult to provide a water dish to small tarantulas, but a spider with a leg span of a 50-cent piece or so is large enough for a simple tiny water receptacle such as a soda bottle cap.

Provide clean tap water in a heavy shallow dish that is smaller in diameter

Some Plants Suitable for Naturalistic Terrariums

Pothos
Sansevieria (snake plant or mother-in-law's tongue)
Swedish ivy
Philodendron
Neoregelia bromeliads

than the tarantula's leg span. A rock can be placed in the dish to prevent crickets or other feeder insects from drowning. Do not use cricket gel or sponges, despite what you may have heard or read elsewhere. Sponges and crystallized water gels just get dirty and contaminated with bacteria and mold and do not provide sufficient hydration.

You can also provide water by lightly misting the substrate and/or sides of the enclosure, but this should not replace the use of a water dish. Never mist or spray the spider directly, and take care to not create overly damp conditions. Most pet tarantulas are grassland or desert species that should have a mostly dry cage, although having a small damp area near the water dish can be helpful. Tropical rainforest species require elevated humidity, and overfilling the water dish each time you refill it to dampen the surrounding substrate may be beneficial. Research your pet's needs and provide accordingly.

Temperature and Heating

Many popular pet tarantulas are burrowers in nature. They live in a

safe chamber at the end of a tubular tunnel that may descend a couple of feet (61 cm) or more into the earth. Here they are protected from

Tarantulas require hiding places in their enclosures. For ground-dwelling species, such as this Honduran Curly Hair (top), you can use a piece of cork bark. Arboreal species, such as the Kandy Highland Ornamental (bottom) do best with vertically oriented hiding places that simulate tree holes. In this enclosure, a hollow piece of bamboo serves this purpose.

Most tarantulas thrive at warm room temperatures, but some rainforest species—including the Cobalt Blue—need a warmer terrarium.

weather and predators, sheltered in a microenvironment with fairly stable temperature and humidity. Even those that dwell in hot dry climates like deserts or savannas survive due to the comparatively mild temperature and elevated humidity within their retreats. This is an important consideration for pet tarantula care—even arid-climate species require some humidity and cannot tolerate excessive heat.

Temperature Range

Many pet tarantulas thrive at room temperatures and require no supplemental heating. If you are comfortable there is a good chance your tarantula will be too. If your room temperatures are on the warm side, such as 72° to 76°F (22.2° to 24.4°C) during the day, your spider should eat regularly and do quite well. If your

home is cooler, supplemental heating may be necessary.

Only truly tropical species like the pink-toed tarantulas (*Avicularia*), goliath bird-eaters (*Theraphosa*) and some of the Asian "earth tigers" like Cobalt Blues (*Haplopelma lividum*) enjoy warmer temperatures. These warmer temperatures are only 78° to 82°F (25.6° to 27.8°C) during the daytime and slightly cooler at night. Temperatures greater than 84°F (29°C) are inappropriate for all tarantulas, and keeping tarantulas in the upper 70s and low 80s (25° to 29°C) requires special diligence by the keeper to ensure that the tarantula has constant access to fresh water and that food is offered at a greater frequency due to the accelerated digestion and increased activity levels that result from warmer temperatures.

Cage Environments for Popular Tarantula Species

Scientific Name	Common Name	Habits	Temperature	Humidity
Acanthoscurria geniculata	Brazilian White-Knee	terrestrial	75-80°F (24-27°C)	65-75%
Aphonopelma seemanni	Stripe-Knee	burrowing	72-76°F (22-24°C)	50-60%
Avicularia avicularia	Common Pink-Toe	arboreal	75-80°F (24-27C)	70-80%
Brachypelma smithi	Mexican Red-Knee	burrowing	72-76°F (22-24°C)	50-70%
Chromatopelma cyaneopubescens	Greenbottle Blue	terrestrial	72-78°F (22-26°C)	40-50%
Grammostola porteri ("rosea")	Chilean Rose	burrowing	70-76°F (21-24°C)	60-70%
Lasiodora parahybana	Brazilian Salmon-Pink	terrestrial	74-78°F (23-26°C)	60-70%
Haplopelma lividum	Cobalt Blue	burrowing	75-78°F (24-26°C)	70-80%
Nhandu chromatus	Brazilian Red and White	burrowing	75-78°F (24-26°C)	60-75%
Pelinobius muticus	King Baboon	burrowing	75-80°F (24-27°C)	65-75%
Phormictipus cancerides	Haitian Brown	terrestrial	75-78°F (24-26°C)	60-75%
Poecilotheria regalis	Indian Ornamental	arboreal	75-78°F (24-26°C)	60-75%
Psalmopoeus irminia	Venezuelan Suntiger	arboreal	75-78°F (24-26°C)	70-80%
Pterniochilus murinus	Orange Baboon	terrestrial	75-78°F (24-26°C)	50-70%
Theraphosa blondi	Goliath Bird-Eater	burrowing	77-82°F (25-28°C)	80-90%

So how do you know whether your tarantula cage is warm enough? Observe your tarantula's behavior. Is it feeding regularly and fasting only when a molt is approaching? Then the temperatures it is exposed to are probably appropriate. Appetite is the best indicator of whether conditions are good. If your tarantula is reluctant to feed or refuses food altogether, and you are certain it is not just fasting because of its molt cycle, you may need to heat its enclosure.

Along with paying attention to your tarantula's behavior and appetite to gauge whether its cage temperatures are adequate, you should also research its natural habitat. Is it a rainforest, grassland, or desert species? Is it an arboreal, terrestrial or fossorial tarantula? As mentioned above, most popular pet tarantulas live in burrows where the temperature range is stable and mild, and these tarantulas often thrive at room temperature. This includes the familiar Chilean Rose-Hair (*Grammostola porteri*), the red-legged tarantulas of the Pacific coast including the familiar Mexican Red-Knee (*Brachypelma smithi*), and the Brazilian Black (*Grammostola pulchra*). In fact, almost all *Aphonopelma*, *Brachypelma*, *Ceratogyrus*, *Grammostola*, and *Pterinochilus* will do fine in unheated cages. Other tarantula hobbyist favorites like the Greenbottle Blue (*Chromatopelma cyaneopubescens*) also adapt to room temperature enclosures.

Terrestrial and arboreal tarantulas are exposed to a wider range of temperatures and humidity levels than burrowing species. Without the microenvironment created by a burrow, their environment tends to fluctuate more. Some arboreal tarantulas, like the *Avicularia* pink-toe tree spiders, are found in equatorial rainforests that are mostly warm and humid. Others, like the ornamental tarantulas of the genus *Poecilotheria*, live where monsoon weather patterns cause wet and dry seasons and variances in temperature. It is essential to thoroughly research the temperature and humidity ranges that keepers have found to be best for the captive care of your species.

As a general rule, the vast majority of tarantula species can be kept in terrariums in the 72° to 78°F range (22.2° to 25.6°C). Many grassland and desert species will do fine at temperatures that fall slightly below that range, although their appetite and activity level will be reduced. Some rainforest species thrive best at the upper end of the aforementioned range or a few degrees above to a maximum daytime high of about 82°F (27.8°C). A fluctuating temperature is best for most tarantulas, with nights cooler than days.

Heating

Although many tarantulas thrive without supplemental heat, it may become necessary to heat your tarantula enclosure, at least during the colder months. This is easily accomplished for most small terrariums by using the miniature size (approximately 4 x 5 inches [10.2 x 12.7 cm] and 4 watts) of heat mats

Tarantula enclosure with an undertank heat mat, thermometer, hygrometer, and cage furnishings.

popular in the reptile hobby. For larger enclosures or collections, other means of heating may be necessary.

External Heating

Many tarantula enthusiasts also keep reptiles, and placing tarantula terrariums in a room also containing heated herp cages is often all that is needed to provide appropriate warmth. You might be able to achieve the same effect by keeping your tarantula in the warmest room in the house.

A method that is popular in Europe but hasn't become common in the United States is to house a number of enclosures in large heated cabinets. This is sort of like taking a large reptile cage and using it as a climate-controlled cupboard for a collection of small cages contained within. This is an excellent set-up for medium-size tarantula collections. Cabinets may be heated with radiant heat panels or heat cable running down the back or beneath shelves. Some cabinets are heated with reptile lamps that do not give off visible light, such as ceramic heat emitters or infrared bulbs. The heating devices are often controlled by a pulse-proportional thermostat that increases or decreases power to the heat source without turning it completely off. You will usually need to purchase these thermostats separately; you can find them at retailers that specialize in reptiles and reptile products.

For those keepers with very large collections, a dedicated room or walk-in closet is ideal. Heat the tarantula

Living Alone

Tarantulas are solitary creatures and are opportunistic predators that will not hesitate to prey upon one of their own. With the exception of a few types that live in communal groups in nature, this means that tarantulas must be housed individually—only one spider per cage. Keepers who are interested in raising tarantulas in groups are limited to spiders such as the ornamental tarantulas (*Poecilotheria*), spiderlings of which may be raised together to adulthood as long as they begin their life in a group. Other possibilities include some pink-toed tarantulas (*Avicularia*)—but definitely not *A. versicolor*—*Holothele*, and *Heterothele* species, and *Hysterocrates*, a genus of large African tarantulas that have been found living in somewhat social groups. In these species multiple generations may feed in proximity to their mother, the youngest sucking juices from the female's prey. Even with these species, it is safest for beginning keepers to house tarantulas singly.

room with a space heater to keep it at 75° to 78°F (24° to 25.6°C) by day and in the low 70s (21° to 23°C) at night. This is an optimal temperature range for keeping and breeding most tarantulas.

Heat Mats

Small heat mats make the best heat sources for individual tarantula enclosures; you find them at most pet stores. These thin plastic-encased electric heaters are specifically designed for terrarium use. A four-watt 4 x 5-inch (10.2 x 12.7 cm) heat mat makes an excellent heat source for the plastic terrariums, storage containers, and small aquariums used for housing tarantulas. Place this small heat mat under one end of the enclosure, or if you have an arboreal tarantula, mount it to the side of the enclosure. Providing localized heat to one area of an enclosure so that there is a

heat gradient will allow a tarantula to choose its own temperature according to its needs. This is called behavioral thermoregulation.

The reptile heat mats I use come with adhesive-backed rubber feet that can be used to raise a terrarium slightly above the heater so that the bottom of the enclosure is not in direct contact with the mat. The combination of this air gap and the depth of substrate act as a buffer between the tarantula and its heat source. This reduces the intensity of the heat—important because tarantulas require more moderate temperatures than the reptiles these products are designed for. Use a thermostat to control the heat mat and verify the temperature with a digital thermometer. Many of these thermometers have an external probe that can be situated where the tarantula spends most of its time or placed in the center of the enclosure to provide an average between the warm end and the cooler end.

Bulbs

It is also possible to heat larger terrariums with bulbs that do not emit visible light (infrared or black reptile heat lamps) or ceramic heat emitters that give off no light at all. Regular light bulbs or heat lamps should not be used. Ultraviolet "black" lights are not suitable for heating terrariums and should not be confused with the black reptile heat lamps found in the pet trade.

Tarantulas are nocturnal and secretive. They shun light. Using bright lights to heat your tarantula's cage will cause stress. Diffuse fluorescent light is fine for planted terrariums that require more than room light, but otherwise direct light should be avoided.

The problem with using radiant bulbs like ceramic emitters and infrared reptile lamps is that they provide dry heat that lowers enclosure humidity and creates an excessively warm hot spot a tarantula doesn't need. Tarantulas don't bask the way lizards do. If you must use this form of terrarium heat, choose the lowest-wattage lamp possible that still provides sufficient heat. For safety, use a fixture with a ceramic socket (not plastic) and a thermostat that will turn the lamp off should temperatures exceed 80°F (26.7°C). When using a heat lamp, you will need to pay extra attention to cage humidity, substrate moisture, and water dish levels.

Humidity and Moisture

Humidity is a measure of the amount of moisture in the air and is expressed as a percentage, with 100 percent noting saturation. Humidity is essential for tarantula health and tarantulas' book lung method of respiration.

Ambient humidity, that of the air in your home, fluctuates during the year and is often lower in the winter due to the methods used to heat our dwellings. Regardless of season, it is often necessary to increase the humidity in your tarantula terrarium so it falls within your species' optimal range.

Methods for Maintaining Humidity

The two best ways to increase terrarium humidity are wetting the substrate and misting. Either way, you are actually adding moisture, not humidity The evaporation of that moisture creates an increase in humidity. One reason to always have a water dish in your tarantula cages is that even this water will over time elevate humidity within the enclosure.

Substrate Moisture

I am a proponent of using the greatest depth of substrate you can based on the height of your cage. There are two reasons for this. One is to minimize cage height to reduce the risk of a falling injury. The second reason relates to humidity and moisture levels: being able to have substrate that is moisture stratified. Being moisture stratified means there are layers of substrate of varying dampness. If you have several inches or more of coconut coir at the bottom of your tarantula's cage, you can run water down one cage wall so that the lower level is fairly damp while the upper inch (2.5 cm) or so is barely moist. Moisture from the bottom of the substrate will evaporate over time and increase the humidity without causing the ground the tarantula lives upon to become wet.

To further explain this concept, we can look at methods used by keepers of other terrarium pets. For example, dart frog keepers create terrariums that have a drainage layer of pebbles or the clay aggregate used in hydroponic gardens beneath a deep depth of soil substrate or layers of earth and moss. This drainage base is typically full of water that is continuously evaporating, moistening the substrate above and adding humidity to the air. Often a vertical tube or pipe is part of the terrarium design. It is used to maintain the desired water level at the bottom of the terrarium by allowing the keeper to add water (often poured through a

The Essential Inexpensive Gauge

Keepers of terrarium pets often talk about whether their tarantula or other critter is warm enough or whether the humidity is sufficient, especially when they are frustrated by the pet's reluctance to feed. Yet when you ask what the cage temperature is they reply with vague responses like "pretty warm." There are handy and inexpensive digital thermometer and hygrometer (humidity gauge) units that can be affixed to the inside of the terrarium. Several reptile product manufacturers produce these items. Of course, similar gauges designed for home use can be found at home centers and hardware stores for about the same price. Make this investment. You can't keep your pets within their optimal temperature and humidity ranges without being able to measure and monitor the levels.

funnel that attaches to the top of the tube or pipe) without having to allow it to percolate through all the levels of substrate, thereby wetting the upper layers. Evaporation of moisture added to the substrate and water from a cage dish is essential for cage humidity.

Misting

Simulating rainfall in your tarantula's cage will both increase the humidity and allow droplets of water to collect and provide drinking water. Misting is unnecessary for many pet tarantulas and improper for arid-climate species, but a fine warm-water mist is useful in tropical terrariums and for quickly revitalizing cage moisture. It is also a great way to provide drinking water to tarantulas that are too small for a water dish. When misting, use lukewarm water and avoid directly spraying the spider.

Ventilation

Keeping the popular pet tarantulas—most of which are grassland or scrubland species—is comparatively easy. These species require well-ventilated enclosures like aquariums with a screen top. For moisture you provide a shallow water bowl and overflow it when you add water so that there is a little moisture in one small area of the substrate that will evaporate over a few days. However, keeping rainforest species that need higher humidity can become more of a challenge.

Good airflow should never be sacrificed in an attempt to maintain elevated humidity. Stagnant conditions probably kill more tarantulas than dryness. This certainly is the case when rearing spiderlings or young tarantulas. Poor ventilation and excessive dampness cause mold and bacteria to thrive and also attracts pests. It is much easier to add moisture when needed than to correct overly swampy cages. Would you rather remoisten the substrate every day or two and give one end of the cage a misting once or twice a week, or have to tear down a planted tropical

Using a deep substrate in a tarantula cage helps retain humidity levels. A Stripe-Knee Tarantula is shown here.

terrarium and recreate it with drier substrate?

Maintenance

A tarantula enclosure needs a complete cleaning only a few times a year. Tarantula waste is a grayish-white paste that can go almost unnoticed, and if the keeper is diligent at removing uneaten food and the remains of prey and regularly cleans the water dish, there is little reason to break down and completely overhaul the enclosure. Keepers of arboreal species may wish to clean their enclosures a bit more frequently, because these tarantulas will defecate on the glass and make their homes more unsightly. Tarantulas like the security of their homes, and many create silken retreats over time and are, therefore, best left undisturbed.

Feeding

Tarantulas will eat crickets, grasshoppers, katydids, moths, beetle larvae (e.g., mealworms or superworms), houseflies, cockroaches, and a host of other arthropods. Most of this insect prey is readily available in pet stores. Some tropical tarantulas eagerly accept earthworms, an often-overlooked but excellent food for large burrowing tarantulas. Larger tarantulas may eat nestling rodents, lizards, and snakes in the wild, but vertebrate prey is completely unnecessary for captive tarantulas. A live rodent can injure your tarantula, and the considerable amount of time it takes even the largest spider to ingest something like a mouse results in a decaying prey item that attracts pests and introduces a foul-smelling mess to the terrarium. Feeding live rodents to arachnids is no different from feeding live rodents to snakes. It is an unnecessary risk of injury to a wonderful predator in an unnatural captive situation where it has no chance for escape. If you want to offer a larger meal to your spider, try roaches instead of rodents.

Prey Size

When feeding, a good rule of thumb is to offer prey items that are about half the spider's leg span or just slightly smaller than the length of its body. For example, a 2-inch (5 cm) leg span juvenile tarantula with a body length of about an inch (2.5 cm) can be offered a ¾-inch (1.9 cm) cricket (four to five weeks old). However, some tarantulas are aggressive eaters and will eat prey as large as themselves. When using comparatively small prey such as crickets to feed adult tarantulas, the aforementioned sizing doesn't work. Instead, offer four or five large crickets to a spider the size of an adult Chilean Rose-Hair (*Grammostola porteri*) or Mexican Red-Knee (*Brachypelma smithi*). It will pounce on them one at a time, filling its jaws with a number of crickets in succession. Eventually it will drop the clump of crickets and use a bit of silk to wrap it into one tidy package that it will resume macerating. This ball of prey wrapped in silk, or bolus, will be ingested over time. After the meal is finished, the bolus will consist mostly of prey exoskeleton and silk and should be removed.

Feeding Frequency

How often you feed your tarantula is up to you. Some people want their spider to grow as fast as possible and will offer food almost every day. However, offering food every four to seven days for young spiders and every ten days to two weeks for larger specimens is a reasonable regimen.

Spiders, in general, will keep eating until they are full, unless they are approaching a molt or ready to lay an egg sac. In a sense, you can't really overfeed young tarantulas, but this isn't the case with adults. An adult tarantula might eat only once a month or even as little as a few times a year in the wild. A tarantula's opisthosoma should not be overly

Crickets are the most common food for pet tarantulas, but the spiders will eat almost any of the available feeder insects.

large; its abdomen should never impede its ability to move about with ease.

Fasting

Novice tarantula keepers often are overly concerned when their tarantulas refuse food, especially hobbyists whose introduction to tarantulaculture is the Chilean Rose-Hair. This species is notorious for fasting. A healthy adult tarantula can go months without food. If food is refused, an impending molt is the most likely reason. Offer food every few weeks and remove it promptly if uneaten. Ensure that fresh water is available and wait for your tarantula's appetite to return.

Uneaten Food

It is extremely important to remove any uneaten prey items whether live or dead within 24 hours or so. I recommend offering food late at night and removing it first thing in the morning if not accepted. Uneaten insects or other prey items can be stressful for the tarantula and have

been known to damage and even kill tarantulas. Food remains like the bolus will attract pests and mold. It is advisable to remove the remains of any prey items so that they do not cause unhealthy conditions for your pet.

Crickets

The domestic cricket is the staple food item for pet tarantulas. Crickets are inexpensive and easy to find at pet stores and bait shops. They are sold in the pet trade in seven sizes from pinhead to fully winged, and most stores stock at least two or three sizes. For the keeper with one tarantula or a very small collection, there is no reason to look far beyond the cricket for tarantula food. For those with more spiders to feed, the cons of cricket use (short life span, high mortality, and the pests attracted to dead crickets as well as their odor and chirping) usually begin to outweigh the convenience.

Mealworms

Alongside the domestic cricket, the pet trade has embraced two "worms" that aren't really worms at all as feeder insects for arachnids and

reptiles. These are the larvae of two types of darkling beetle, the mealworm and superworm. The mealworm (*Tenebrio molitor*) is now available in a few sizes, and a related species of mini-mealworm (*T. obscurus*) is sometimes found. The superworm (also called king mealworm, *Zophobas morio*) is a larger grub and can be an excellent food for tarantulas.

The problem with both the mealworm and superworm is that they will not roam around the terrarium like a cricket or roach. Unless the tarantula pounces on it immediately, a beetle grub will burrow into the substrate and escape detection. More often than not, it will stay where it digs and later pupate to become a beetle. However, for tarantulas with a quick feeding response, especially young tarantulas

Chilean Rose-Hair feeding on a cockroach. Feeder cockroaches are one of the author's recommended tarantula foods.

housed in small containers where the chance of predator/prey encounter is increased, the use of mealworms or kingworms is extremely convenient.

Mealworms can be refrigerated. They will become dormant, require no feeding, and last for weeks. However, superworms will not tolerate cold and must be kept at room temperature. Place them in a container containing a layer of bran and offer carrot and potato slices and they will last quite a while. When kept in groups they will not pupate.

Roaches

Many arachnid enthusiasts not only raise exotic roaches as food for their animals but also have a great interest in these fascinating creatures and keep them as pets. What roach haters do not realize is that of the thousands of roach species worldwide only a few dozen are actually household pests. These pest species prosper in filthy environments, but roaches are not themselves dirty. Most live on the forest floor, in caves, and in other areas away from human habitation. They are tropical species that can't survive long in our cool, dry homes. They require vegetation and moisture to survive, unlike the household pest roaches that will feed on almost anything, including linoleum and cardboard glue.

A wide variety of roach species are now cultivated in captivity and are readily available to the hobbyist. These species can be split into two groups: those that can climb smooth vertical surfaces such as glass, and those that cannot. A popular example of a glass-climber is *Gromphadorhina portentosa*, the Madagascan hissing roach. This is a popular pet species, but it is avoided by many who breed roaches for food because of its hard exoskeleton and climbing ability. *Nauphoeta cinerea*, commonly known as the lobster roach, is a small climbing roach species that produces babies small enough to feed to tiny tarantula spiderlings and is among the most prolific and hardy roaches in captivity. The roach species I raise and recommend are all large non-climbers: *Blaberus craniifer* (death's head roach), *B. discoidalis* (discoid or false death's head roach), *B. fusca* (brown cave roach), and *Blaptica dubia* (Guyana spotted roach).

No Thanks, I'm Molting

Tarantulas will refuse food for a period of time prior to molting. Do not feed freshly molted young tarantulas for several days, and wait at least one week before offering food to adults. This allows time for the new exoskeleton, including fangs and mouthparts, to harden.

Review of Food Choices

FOOD	PROS	CONS
Crickets	Inexpensive and readily available at pet stores and bait shops in many different sizes. This is the number one tarantula food source.	Short life span and a hassle to keep due to feeding, maintenance, odor, and, for fully winged adults, noise.
Mealworms and Superworms	Very convenient. Regular mealworms may be refrigerated and superworms are easy to care for.	Will burrow so they disappear if the tarantula does not attack immediately.
Roaches	The serious tarantula keeper's number one food source.	Many people have a dislike for roaches and don't want them in their homes.
Nightcrawlers and other earthworms	Eagerly accepted by tropical tarantulas, especially larger species. Inexpensive and easy to store for weeks.	Will burrow if not immediately eaten and will not survive unless substrate is very damp. The use of farmed/cultured worms is recommended, as wild worms consume soil in yards and gardens that may be treated with chemicals.
Waxworms	Available in bait shops and pet stores.	More expensive than beetle larvae and harder to keep alive. Healthy and warm waxworms will encase themselves in silk and pupate and be hard to use. Do not live long when refrigerated.
Fruit Flies	Flightless fruit flies are easy to culture and good for tiny spiders (but few tarantulas).	Very few spiderling tarantulas are so small that fruit flies are an appropriate food. Escapees are a nuisance.
Grasshoppers and Katydids	If you find these around your home and you can collect them from an area untreated by pesticides or other chemicals they are a great free food source.	Must be field-collected and may have been exposed to chemicals.

NOT IN USE	REASON	
Moths, Butterflies, Caterpillars	Moths can be a good food source, especially for arboreal tarantulas, but some species are poisonous. The greater wax moth, the larvae of which are sold as waxworms, is fine. Cultured caterpillars like silkworms and tomato hornworms are also safe. However, unless you are certain you can identify those that are harmless, it is best to avoid other moths, butterflies, and their caterpillars.	
Beetles	Same as above. Some species are poisonous and some are predatory and may injure your tarantula. The beetles that mealworms and kingworms morph into are okay, but they secrete a defensive chemical with a sickly odor and are rejected by most tarantulas	
Rodents and other vertebrates	As discussed in this chapter, there is no reason to feed a rodent or other vertebrate to a tarantula and risk injury. Roaches make a far superior large meal. It takes a long time for a tarantula to ingest something like a mouse, and the odor and mess it causes and the pest flies it may attract are undesirable.	

Nightcrawlers

It is surprising how many tarantula keepers overlook using nightcrawlers and other earthworms as food for tarantulas. Worms of all sorts account for a good portion of the natural diet of many types of tarantulas, especially tropical burrowing species that will encounter worms quite often. Nightcrawlers are relished by many of the larger South American tarantulas like *Megaphobema*, *Pamphobeteus*, *Theraphosa*, and *Xenesthis*. I have personally observed (by using an endoscope to view deep inside their burrows) the Costa Rican species *Megaphobema mesomelas* and *Sphaerobothria hoffmani* feeding on large worms. A colleague who has had great success with the captive breeding of the aforementioned tarantulas credits his use of nightcrawlers for keeping these spiders in prime condition. Smaller earthworms are good for smaller specimens and may be cut to feed several spiders.

Of course, worms will burrow if given the chance and are best offered to tarantulas with an eager appetite. They are also soft and moist and will not do well in drier tarantula enclosures if not immediately eaten. Because they consume earth that may be treated with weed killers, pesticides, or fertilizers, garden worms or nightcrawlers found around your home should be avoided. It is best to obtain cultured worms from a bait shop or pet store.

Feeding Burrowing Prey

Offer mealworms, nightcrawlers, and other prey items that burrow using long forceps so you disturb the tarantula as little as possible while you drop the meal directly in front of it. Otherwise, the mealworm, nightcrawler, or other burrower may burrow into the substrate and escape its fate.

Waxworms

The greater wax moth or honeycomb moth (*Galleria mellonella*) is an excellent tarantula food, both in the larval form (sold as waxworms) and as the adult moth. Waxworms are particularly well suited for rearing a large number of young arboreal tarantulas. The difficulty with waxworms is that they are usually packaged in sawdust and refrigerated to prevent their metamorphosis to moths. They do not live long housed like this, so buy only what you can use right away. If you want to raise them to moths they need to be kept warm (80 to 85°F [26.7 to 29.4°C]) and provided with food. Wax moth larvae feed on beeswax, and discarded honeycombs are sold in health food stores and country shops. Place the waxworms in a mix of rolled oats and honeycomb and they will pupate in a month or so.

A Final Word on Feeding

Tarantulas may do well feeding on nothing but crickets for many years.

However, varying the diet certainly cannot harm the tarantula and may contribute to improved health. I suggest trying new feeder insects every now and then. I definitely recommend that keepers who intend to breed their tarantulas offer a wide variety of prey and use insects that have been gut-loaded by offering nutritious foods for several days. In fact, all keepers should ensure that their tarantulas receive healthy prey that has been provided with ample food and water prior to offering.

Molting

Tarantulas are invertebrate animals that need to shed their complete exoskeleton in order to grow. This is the time when the tarantula is at its most vulnerable. Molting may occur as often as once a month in young

In nature, tarantulas occasionally eat frogs, lizards, and other small vertebrates. However, providing such food to pet tarantulas is problematic.

spiderlings or only once every year or two in adults.

Preparing for the Molt

As a molt approaches, the tarantula may refuse food, sometimes for several weeks or even months prior to the process. If your tarantula refuses several offered meals in a row it may be about to molt. Further evidence of an impending molt is reduced activity, increased use of silk as it creates a molting mat, and dull coloration.

It is easy to assess the molting status of species that flick urticating hairs and develop a bald spot on the abdomen. The light bald spot will become

increasingly dark until it is almost black just prior to molting.

If you believe your tarantula will soon molt it is extra important to make sure you remove uneaten food—you should always be doing this anyway—and pay close attention to temperature and humidity levels. A slight increase in humidity is recommended (add water to substrate at one end of cage and keep water dish full) during the molting period. Leave the tarantula undisturbed, and certainly do not touch or handle it.

The Molting Process

When a terrestrial tarantula molts it will turn onto its back. Don't be alarmed—it is not dead. Dead tarantulas usually are right side up and have their legs curled beneath their bodies. Arboreal tarantulas molt on their backs or sides, often in a silken retreat above the ground where they may be vertical.

As the tarantula lies inverted, a pumping action caused by an increase in heart rate creates pressure within its body and begins to separate the old exoskeleton from the new cuticle that has formed beneath. First the carapace loosens and is pushed away. Then the tarantula will pull its legs out of its old skin much as you pull your fingers out of a glove. The cast-off exoskeleton (or *exuvium*) looks much like a hollowed-out complete tarantula. The entire process may take as little as 30 minutes but may take as long as a couple of days, especially in elderly tarantulas.

Once the process is completed the pale-colored tarantula will rest for as

You Are What You Eat

Keepers of insectivorous lizards have become very aware that providing the crickets and other feeder insects with nutritious foods is essential to their lizards' health. Although some might argue that tarantulas don't have the nutritional requirements of vertebrates, your spider can only benefit from consuming well-fed prey that has been gut-loaded. Gut-loading refers to the practice of feeding prey insects healthy foods and offering plenty of water for at least 24 hours prior to using them as food. For crickets, dark leafy greens like turnip, collard, and mustard are the best fresh foods to use, and several reptile product companies offer dry gut-loading diets. You can provide crickets moisture by giving them slices of potato, apple, orange, or similar fruits.

much as a day and then spend the next week or so with its legs outstretched as its growing process occurs and its new exoskeleton hardens. Do not disturb or feed your tarantula for at least a week after molting. Young tarantulas may fully harden in three or four days, but an adult may require two weeks. It is extremely delicate at this time and can even be injured by attempting to flick urticating hairs off its soft abdomen. Leave it alone.

Raising Young Tarantuas

Raising young tarantulas is among the most rewarding aspects of the hobby. Watching young captive-bred theraphosid spiders grow from a speck to perhaps the size of your hand, and witnessing the gradual transformation of coloration and pattern, quickly becomes a favorite experience. For many keepers the experience is addictive, and the small space needed for a number of deli-cup tarantula nurseries soon is filled with an assortment of species and maybe hundreds of rearing jars.

Keeping spiderlings is not just for seasoned keepers. Keepers of all levels are experiencing the joys of raising young tarantulas. With the information found in this section even the neophyte enthusiast can enjoy the thrilling pursuit of raising future big and hairy spiders.

The Basics

Many people are surprised to discover just how small many "giant spiders" can be. The Brazilian Salmon-Pink (*Lasiodora parahybana*) reaches a size that rivals even the three species of bird-eaters (*Theraphosa apophysis, T. blondi,* and *T. stirmi*), yet it begins life with a leg span less than 0.25 inch

Molting of a Mexican Fire-Leg tarantula. Tarantulas begin molting on their backs and slowly extract themselves from the old exoskeleton.

(6.3 mm). The reproductive strategy of *L. parahybana* is to have a very large number of young (often in excess of 2000 nymphs), few of which survive to adulthood. However, the three species of *Theraphosa* have closer to 100 offspring, and these begin their lives with a leg span of 1 inch (2.5 cm) or more and a bit more of a fighting chance. Overall, early instar tarantulas (spiderlings) are about 0.25 to 0.5 inches (6.3-12.7 mm) in diagonal leg span, slightly larger in some arboreal species and much smaller for some dwarfs.

So how do we keep these mini-tarantulas alive? It's easier than most inexperienced keepers believe. With a small escape-proof container, plenty of food, and a touch of humidity, most captive-bred spiderling tarantulas thrive. Raising spiderlings requires frequent feeding to keep the tarantulas both nourished and hydrated. As you will learn below, finding food for your spiderlings is easy.

This three-year-old Mexican Fire-Leg is an ideal choice for a beginning keeper who wants to enjoy raising a juvenile tarantula to adulthood.

Buy Captive Bred

Most terrarium pets now sold have been bred in captivity, and tarantulas are no exception. Global captive breeding efforts have reduced the pressure on wild populations and their habitat and contributed enormously to the surge in the popularity of tarantula keeping. Choosing a captive-bred tarantula will reward you with a stronger, healthier pet and benefit the spiders living in nature.

Housing Spiderlings
A mini terrarium for a spiderling need be nothing more than a baby food jar with air holes drilled in the lid. I used hundreds of these 30 years ago with great success. Today, clear plastic vials have become the most popular container for rearing tarantula spiderlings, but a number of food storage containers and craft shop transparent enclosures can also be adapted as tarantula nurseries.

Enclosures
The most important thing to consider when choosing housing for your spiderling is that it provides both security and some degree of elevated humidity without sacrificing ventilation. Small container size will not only give the tarantula a snug and protected lair in which it can easily locate its prey but also make it easier for you to monitor feeding and molting. It is important to

Your Pet Tarantula

ensure that uneaten food is removed promptly, especially during a molt cycle. A hungry cricket can harm a tarantula that is refusing food due to the impending molt or, worse still, is in the molting process and too vulnerable to protect itself.

The most popular spiderling rearing container is the plastic vial. Twenty-dram to fifty-dram vials are most popular, and the larger sizes can accommodate spiderlings up to 1 inch (2.5 cm) or more in leg span. Vials allow a good depth of substrate, so the spiderling can burrow, which reduces the risk of desiccation. The transparent crystal polystyrene vials favored by most tarantula keepers allow for easy viewing as long as the spiderling is not burrowed.

Other suitable containers include baby food jars and 1-oz. to 3-oz (30 to 88.7 ml) plastic condiment cups. A clear acrylic container that I like to use for terrestrial tarantulas is actually designed for displaying a toy car (such as Matchbox or Hot Wheels). Create ventilation to any of these containers by adding a number of very small holes to the lid. Vials come with soft snap caps that you can easily pierce with a miniature Phillips screwdriver or a nail. Other plastic enclosures can be modified with a series of drilled holes that allow for flow of air. Be careful that any air holes do not permit the spider's escape. Spiders can pass through surprisingly small holes, so make sure that holes have a diameter no more than half the thickness of the tarantula's widest point.

Setting Up

Let's assume that you have purchased a

Plastic vials and deli cups make excellent mini-terrariums for spiderlings and juveniles.

spiderling of a terrestrial or burrowing species. You have done some research and asked questions of other keepers on Internet forums and chosen a species of interest. You've found a clean baby food jar and have drilled a dozen tiny holes in the lid for ventilation. Or maybe you have a clear vial with poked holes.

The next step is to fill the container about half way with some type of substrate. Garden soil, top soil, and potting soil as well as peat moss, horticultural vermiculite, and coconut coir are the substrates most keepers use. Any of these substrates or a combination of them works well. I like coconut coir and mix it with vermiculite in a ratio of two parts coir to one part vermiculite. Adding vermiculite to the coir improves moisture retention and drainage. It also allows the substrate to hold its form better, providing better structural integrity to burrows.

I moisten the mixture by gradually adding tepid water while stirring with a trowel. If you have a small terrarium, you may need to do the mixing in another container and then add the mixture to the enclosure. The substrate should clump slightly when squeezed in a fist. If you can easily squeeze water out, the mix is too wet. In this case, you will need to add more substrate to dry the mix until it will barely clump together. You may need to adjust the moisture content of the substrate for species that require particularly dry or moist conditions, but it is best to err on the side of dryness while trying

Many species of tarantulas go through a dramatic color change during their lives, and watching this change is part of the joy of raising baby spiders. For example, spiderling Antilles Pink-Toes (top) are brilliant blue, while the adults (bottom) are maroon, green, and black.

Housing for a young tarantula made from a 24-oz (0.7-l) deli cup with an insect lid designed for fruit fly cultures and a substrate of coir and sphagnum moss.

to achieve the perfect balance. Even spiderlings of Asian species that live in deep burrows in humid jungles will die from excessively damp conditions. Experience has taught many keepers the hard lesson that even these jungle dwellers quickly succumb to wet and stagnant conditions.

Once the jar or vial is filled halfway, tamp down the substrate so it is well compacted. You can create a starter burrow by using the tip of a pencil or something similar to make a 1-inch (2.5-cm) deep hole down the side of the container. This creates a shelter that many spiderlings will retreat into and expand into a larger tunnel over time. The confines of this burrow will keep the spider secure and help protect it from drying out. Placing the hole near the side of the container may allow you to see the spiderling even when it is in the burrow.

Humidity and Moisture

Spiderlings will acquire most of the water they need from their prey. From time to time they will drink from water droplets formed in their container during misting or substrate remoistening (see Watering and Feeding section below). At this stage of their lives they are often too small to be given a water dish. As the spider grows, or if you obtained a larger juvenile specimen, a good first water dish is a 2-liter soda bottle cap. As a rule, the water container's diameter should be less than the leg span of the spider. For tarantulas with a diagonal leg span of 1.5 inches (3.8 cm) or larger a soda bottle cap is the appropriate size for a water bowl; do not offer a tarantula that is smaller than this a water bowl because of the risk of drowning.

Temperature

Tarantula spiderlings need roughly the same temperatures as the adults, so warm room temperatures (72° to 78°F [22.2 to 25.6°C]) are sufficient for raising most species. For rainforest species that need a bit more warmth, it is best to house one or more spiderling containers in a larger heated enclosure that acts as sort of an incubator. For example, an aquarium may be equipped with an under-tank reptile heat mat that is regulated by a thermostat to warm the air in the tank to 75° to 80°F (24° to 26.7°C). Room temperatures around the tank will fluctuate from day to night and allow for some variance in warmth. Spiderling jars are then placed on some type of riser or shelf that keeps them above contact with the heated floor of the tank. In this self-contained warm cabinet—a theraphosid maternity ward of sorts—you can control the climate of a number of individual spiderling containers.

Deli-Cup Style Containers for Larger Spiders

As spiderlings outgrow vial-type containers they can be transferred to larger homes such as clear 3.5-inch (8.9-cm) diameter deli cups of 16 or 24 oz (0.5 or 0.7 l) volume for terrestrial species and 32 oz (0.9 l) for arboreal species. These containers can be found in supermarkets and many restaurants.

If you ask a store or restaurant manager whether you can buy some, they may just give you a few at no cost. Larger quantities may be purchased at cash-and-carry restaurant supply stores or warehouse clubs. You may add ventilation holes to these grocery store

An Ideal Container for Young Tarantulas

A deli cup with an insect lid is an excellent enclosure for tarantulas ranging from 1 to 3 inches (2.5 to 7.6 cm) in leg span. At Tarantulas.com we use 3.5-inch (8.9-cm)/24-oz (0.7-l) diameter cups for terrestrial and small arboreal tarantulas and use 32-oz (0.9-l) for most arboreal spiderlings and a few other species like Greenbottle Blues. At least 2 inches (5 cm) of a moist soil and vermiculite mix is placed in the bottom, and the surface is covered with a half-inch of damp orchid (sphagnum) moss. When the cups are first made they feel relatively heavy with water, but it evaporates over one week's time, and more water is then added to renew the cycle of hydration and evaporation.

An arboreal spiderling, such as this Venezuelan Suntiger, needs a bit of silk plant or other climbing material in its terrarium.

containers or purchase pre-ventilated clear cups from reptile product dealers.

Also available from reptile stores and fruit fly breeders is a special ventilated fabric insect lid that fits these cups. This type of lid is primarily used for fruit fly cultures and provides significantly better ventilation than air holes added to vials and similar small containers. An added benefit of the insect-style lid is that it prevents tiny flies and other pests from entering your tarantula's home.

These recommended cup sizes allow for a generous depth of substrate. Having a greater volume of substrate allows you to safely add more moisture and add it less often. In effect you can add water so that you achieve a gradient from mostly dry surface to fairly damp bottom. By pouring water slowly down the side of the cup—trying to keep most of the surface dry while the water percolates to the bottom layers of substrate—a reservoir of wet substrate will form that can evaporate over time and provide beneficial humidity.

As you can see, the best conditions for rearing young tarantulas require carefully balancing sufficient moisture with adequate ventilation. There is a cycle of evaporation and rehydration, just as there usually is in nature. The fluctuation in humidity is natural. Remember that it is much easier to add more water than to remove excessive water. Adding moisture regularly and allowing it to evaporate will result in much greater success in raising spiderlings.

Special Considerations for Tree-Dwelling Species

Arboreal species, such as those of the genera *Avicularia* and *Poecilotheria*, will require slightly taller containers such as a 50-dram vial. For these tarantulas the container should be filled only about one third of the way with substrate. You still want to have as much volume of substrate as possible, but these species need to have vertical space. A small sprig of silk plant (for *Avicularia* and *Psalmopoeus* species) or a small piece of bark (for *Poecilotheria*) will provide a climbing surface and retreat. Arboreal tarantulas, especially *Avicularia*, will typically create silken tube retreats at the top of the container.

Lightly misting the enclosure, always avoiding spraying the spider directly, will help maintain humidity for the tropical arboreal tarantula species. Misting once or twice a week should be sufficient, and there should be enough ventilation so that the enclosure dries within a day or two. If the substrate becomes increasingly damp, decrease the frequency or amount of misting and/or increase airflow. Always avoid creating damp and stagnant conditions.

Water

As mentioned above, spiderlings are too small for water dishes and will obtain enough water from their prey as long as the container doesn't become very dry. Once a terrestrial tarantula has a leg span equal to or greater than a 2-liter soda bottle cap something like that can be used as a water dish. Always use fresh water. Do not use cricket

It's critical to supply a spiderling with both proper humidity and good ventilation. This is a juvenile Orange Baboon Tarantula.

gel or damp sponges, paper towels or cotton balls. These quickly become dirty bacteria breeding grounds. If the spider's legs span the water container it will not drown. A stick or stone can be placed in the water to prevent crickets from drowning.

Feeding Spiderlings

The one thing that makes most potential

spiderling keepers nervous is feeding. Many people believe that pinhead crickets—these are freshly hatched, extremely tiny crickets—or fruit flies are necessary. The truth is that most terrestrial and some arboreal tarantula babies will scavenge from dead insects, and you can use freshly killed larger insects as a food source. This is natural behavior for some spiderling tarantulas. Tarantula mothers tend to their egg sacs. The young of many species do not disperse upon hatching, but instead remain in the safety zone of their mother's nest. Here they will gather near the mother's mouth while she is feeding and sometimes snack on her kill. This phenomenon can be exploited by tarantulaculturists who find using larger crickets more convenient. Some

keepers just smash the head of the cricket, while others cut large crickets into a few pieces and offer each to an individual spider. This method of feeding works best with terrestrial tarantulas, especially those that inhabit grasslands, scrubs, and deserts. It is less successful with arboreal tarantulas and some tropical burrowing tarantulas. It is worth trying with any spider when small food is hard to come by.

Prey Size

New keepers tend to underestimate the size of meal a spiderling will be able to consume. As a rule, offer a cricket or other insect that is approximately the total length of the spider's body (excluding legs). Some species are very aggressive feeders and will wrestle a

Greenbottle Blue spiderling eating a cricket inside the silken tube it has made.

cricket as large as their leg span to its death! Greenbottle Blues in particular will do a couple of cartwheels as they subdue a meal as large as themselves. This is one species that likes to make its own kill and doesn't fall for dead cricket pieces.

Arboreal species have slightly larger spiderlings that will usually eat insects as large as their leg span, and they have no difficulty with two- or three-week-old crickets (the "small" size sold by many pet stores).

For very small spiderlings, one-week-old crickets are the right size, and newly hatched pinhead crickets are rarely necessary. Along with small crickets, mini-mealworms, Phoenix worms, small waxworms, and fly maggots can be used to feed early instar tarantulas. Fruit flies are too small for most tarantulas, and even the flightless varieties evade capture more often than not. They are a hassle to deal with, and, thankfully, most keepers will never need them, but if you have a couple of hundred tiny spiderling Costa Rican Tiger-Rumps (*Cyclosternum fasciatum*) to feed you might wish to give them a try.

Feeding Frequency

A good feeding regimen for spiderlings is to offer a single appropriately sized prey item once or twice a week—about every three to seven days. Feeding less frequently will increase the risk of desiccation because early instar tarantulas are acquiring most of their water from their food.

Some keepers like to "power feed" their spiderlings so that they grow

more quickly and will offer food almost daily. Typically these spiders are kept at warmer temperatures (in the low 80s [27° to 29°C]) at which appetite and digestion are accelerated. Whether this practice is detrimental to the health and life span of the spider is not known, but the same practice does have adverse results in other animals such as reptiles. It is true that adult tarantulas can be overfed and become obese, but it is unlikely that harm can come to a spiderling from an abundance of food. Spiderlings usually will self-regulate by ignoring food once their abdomens are full. Once capacity is reached it often is time to molt and grow.

Tarantula abdomen size is a good indicator of how well fed (and hydrated) they are. If the opisthosoma isn't nice and plump after a meal you may need to increase frequency of feeding or size of meal. This visual guide to how often and how much to feed takes the guesswork out of feeding young tarantulas. And close regular inspection of your spider will keep you in tune with its cycle, as you will begin to notice when its color fades and abdomen darkens as a molt approaches.

Tarantulas

Keep Up With the Cleaning

One of the most important things to remember when feeding spiderlings is to remove any uneaten food or remains of prey immediately the following day. The best routine is to offer food at dusk or early evening, leave the tarantula undisturbed overnight, and diligently remove uneaten food or the bolus the next morning. Dead crickets will attract pests and produce odor. A dirty enclosure may grow mold or fungus. Live crickets can injure or kill a spiderling if it is fasting or molting. It is imperative that you monitor your spiderling's eating and keep its container clean.

Molting

Molting occurs with greatest frequency when spiders are young. Therefore it is not unusual for a spiderling to shed every month or two. Since most tarantulas will fast for a period of days or weeks prior to a molt, it follows that it is normal for spiderlings to refuse food every so often. That is usually the sign that a molt is coming. You may also notice its coloration gradually fade as the molt approaches, and just prior to shedding the tarantula's abdomen will become dark and have a dull sheen.

It is essential that you do not offer food at this time. By checking for remaining food every morning after feeding you will be able to prevent the spiderling from being killed by a hungry cricket that nibbles on it during a molt. Wait for at least four days after a molt to offer food again. During this time the spider will grow and its new exoskeleton will harden. The spider will be particularly vulnerable at this time and should be left alone as much as possible. Remove the molted skin as soon as possible after the spider is completely finished molting.

Sexing

Once a tarantula has reached a leg span of around 2 inches (5 cm) an experienced person can determine its sex using a stereo dissecting microscope to look for the absence or presence of spermathecae in the cast skin. For more details on sexing, see Chapter 1.

Handling

Some species of tarantula are known

Moving Spiderlings

Spiderlings should not be handled. They are small, delicate, and too easy to injure or lose. But transferring them to another container is often necessary, as is catching them should they run out of the container during feeding or maintenance. The essential tool for this is a small artist's paintbrush, and cheap plastic brushes can be found at dollar stores. Gently brushing the spider is the best method of gently persuading it to move in the direction you wish. The use of a brush is safe and generally calms the spider rather than irritates it.

for their docile nature and are handled by their keepers. Others have defensive dispositions and are quick to bite. *I do not advocate handling any tarantulas, primarily for the safety of the spider.* Tarantulas are extremely fragile creatures that can easily be injured or killed by a fall or other mishap. Even a fall of a couple of inches can kill a tarantula.

In addition, all tarantulas are venomous and have the ability to bite. Their venom may not be life-threatening, but it can cause severe pain and several days of muscle spasms and cramps or worse. Persons allergic to bee stings or otherwise sensitive to venom may experience particular discomfort, and anaphylactic shock may be a concern. Tarantulas are untamed animals and unpredictable. They are terrarium pets like tropical fish or frogs and are best enjoyed through observation and care, not interaction.

Despite my opinion that tarantulas should not be handled, I realize that a great number of keepers do hold their

tarantulas, and even those who don't wish to handle them do need to move them occasionally. For this reason I must address safe methods of handling tarantulas and then discuss ways to manipulate them without contact.

Safe Handling Techniques

For those who wish to handle their spiders, you should acquire one of the more placid species like a Chaco Gold-Striped or a Mexican Red-Knee. Start by placing the tarantula's terrarium on the floor and sitting next to it. You want to minimize any risk of a tragic fall, and starting on the ground is best. Don't handle your tarantula over a carpeted floor. Although the softness might cushion a fall, there is a chance that the spider's tarsal claws might get caught in carpet fibers.

Gently open the terrarium and lay one hand flat a few inches in front of the tarantula. Use your other hand or a soft tool like a paint brush to gently touch the end of the tarantula's abdomen to cause it to move forward and hopefully walk onto your outstretched hand. Should this work you should keep your hand open and slowly move it toward you, allowing the tarantula to crawl on you as if you were the ground or a tree. Make no attempt to restrain it and do not make any sudden

FAMILY-FRIENDLY TIP

Family Record Keeping

Keeping feeding and molting records is a fun way to track your spiderling's progress. By noting when food is accepted or refused you will begin to predict when molting is likely to occur and anticipate when your tarantula will begin refusing food. Record keeping will help ensure that food is offered regularly, and molting tarantulas are not harmed by their intended prey.

This can be a good way to involve a child in tarantula care. A younger child can mark on a calendar each time a tarantula is fed or molts. Children who like to draw might enjoy making an actual-size portrait to accompany the record. An older child can keep more detailed written or computer records, including things such as leg span, cage cleanings, or any other data you might find useful.

movements. Let it move as it desires.

If you have a tarantula that is very docile and is accustomed to handling you can scoop it up by cautiously sliding each hand, palm up, underneath it from opposite directions. A variation of this is to cup your hand slightly and then lower it quickly, yet gently, over the tarantula as though the spider was an egg you might break. With your index finger draped over the chelicerae to the front and your thumb and middle finger on opposite sides of the tarantula's body you can then grasp the tarantula with very little pressure and smoothly turn your hand up so the spider is resting on its back. This method is good for those who wish to examine the ventral surface of the spider for sexing.

As important as the correct ways to handle a tarantula are the things you must avoid for the safety of both the spider and its handler. Do not squeeze a tarantula or attempt to employ a pinching grasp between its second and third pair of legs, as has been suggested by some authors. Do not use forceps or another tool to pick up a tarantula, and do not grasp it by its legs.

Please remember that most people do not like spiders. You are enlightened and know that tarantulas are fascinating and beautiful and that some can be quite docile, but most of your fellow humans aren't so aware. Never use your tarantula to startle or scare someone. Do not bring it to public places without permission. Thrusting your tarantula into someone's personal space is not good public relations for our hobby and could expose you to civil or criminal legal action. Many people have true arachnophobia, and even those who just dislike spiders aren't going to be converted by the sudden appearance of a big hairy spider. Keep your tarantula in its enclosure and let visitors gradually get comfortable with its presence. Use the time to educate them about tarantula habits and how much you enjoy keeping tarantulas. That will go a long way toward understanding and may even create a new tarantulaculturist.

Non-Contact Manipulation of Tarantulas

My mother loves animals and was one of those rare American housewives who didn't kill every spider that took up residence in a corner of our home. In fact, she didn't kill any, and spared other "bugs" as well. She trapped the spiders and insects using a glass and a piece of card, and then released them outdoors. This is the same method I, and probably many of you, used to capture a myriad of spiders and bugs as a youngster; cover them with a clear glass and slide a card or heavy piece of paper over the glass mouth to carefully trap them inside. This technique also works wonders for moving tarantulas as necessary.

The modification I have made to utilize the glass and card technique for trapping tarantulas to move them without contact is to use plastic soda or water bottles that have had their bottoms cut off. This creates an open

How Do I Know Whether My Tarantula Is Going to Molt?

Prior to molting, a tarantula will often refuse food and become less active. It may hide more than usual. Keepers often notice that a tarantula that rarely lines its cage with silk will create a molting mat or, for some species, a silken retreat. The spider's colors will appear duller. In species that develop bald spots on the abdomen from kicking urticating hairs, this pale spot will darken.

Tarantulas that are about to molt should be left undisturbed, and a newly molted tarantula should remain undisturbed for about a week. Once it has shed it will need time to rest and recover while its soft new skin (which includes the mouth, pharynx, and sucking stomach it needs to feed) hardens. Do not offer food to a freshly molted tarantula.

end similar to that of a glass or jar, but the cut bottle tapers to an opposite end that securely holds the tarantula and has a small opening the tarantula cannot fit through. A 2-liter soda bottle can be used for large tarantulas, while smaller sizes of plastic bottles can be used for smaller specimens. The advantage of the small open end is that once you move the tarantula to its destination you can insert a long-handled artist's paintbrush through the opening to gently coax the tarantula back out of the bottle. The benefit of the tapered shape is that the open end is plenty wide enough to allow for easy entrance, but once the tarantula walks farther inside it is held more securely.

Falls can fatally injure tarantulas, so be very careful when you handle yours.

Tools of the Hobby

There are a number of tools and pieces of equipment that are useful to the tarantula keeper. These tools make handling, transporting, and examining your pet much easier.

The preceding section discussed the soda bottle method of trapping a tarantula; the keeper should make a number of these bottles in sizes appropriate for each tarantula in his or her collection. Having a series of containers like deli cups or margarine tubs to temporarily hold tarantulas is also wise. You can also use these to construct an ICU if needed (see Chapter 4: The Healthy Tarantula).

Also mentioned was the indispensable artist's paintbrush. You can find cheap plastic ones in dollar stores, and I suggest having various sizes. I have brushes that range in size from the thin ones in a child's watercolor paint set to one-inch- (2.5-cm) wide brushes with 2-foot-long (61-cm) handles.

Forceps are used for a number of purposes including feeding, removing uneaten food and prey remains or molts, and moving cork bark or other cage décor while keeping your hands out of harm's way. Keep a number of different sizes readily available, from 6-inch tweezers (15.2-cm) to 24-inch (61-cm) rubber-tipped forceps.

I have found that a small mirror on a telescopic handle (available at auto parts and hardware stores) is very useful for examining tarantulas hidden in burrows or retreats. Also of great use for viewing tarantulas in the terrarium is a powerful LED penlight.

Use a Spotter

It is best to have a helper present in case the tarantula runs up your arm and gets behind you or otherwise attempts to get away. The helper should have a small container and lid handy to catch the tarantula if necessary. The tarantula can be directed into the container using a long-handled artist's paintbrush or something similar, and then placed back into its terrarium.

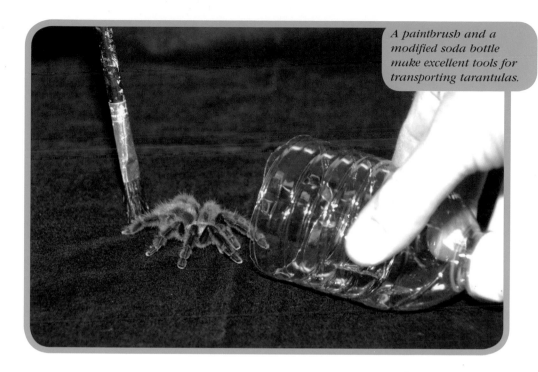

A paintbrush and a modified soda bottle make excellent tools for transporting tarantulas.

For watering tarantulas, a spray bottle and a watering can are needed. Additionally, I like to use eye droppers to add water to small containers used to raise spiderlings, and a turkey baster as a sort of giant eye dropper to add water to larger tarantula enclosures.

Finally, create a first aid kit that contains items for both the keeper and the kept (see chapter 4: The Healthy Tarantula). For the keeper, I recommend two antihistamines to reduce the effects of urticating hair exposure: an oral allergy relief tablet and an anti-itch spray for affected areas. For injuries to tarantulas, such as clotting hemolymph if a leg is pulled off or the tarantula is otherwise wounded, a super glue or liquid bandage is invaluable. As an alternative, corn starch or styptic powder may be used.

Chapter 3

The Healthy

Tarantula

Tarantulas that adjust to captivity and are housed within an optimal temperature and humidity range have very few health issues. Captive-bred specimens suffer few health problems, and even wild-caught specimens will typically acclimate if their environment is correct. The truth is that tarantula keepers see so few health problems that we know very little about treating those that might occur. This chapter covers some of the ailments of captive tarantulas and the remedies that may correct them.

Dehydration

The most common problem seen in captive tarantulas is dehydration. Wild-caught tarantulas are housed in terrible conditions before they reach the pet store. They are often packed into tiny dry cups with a useless piece of once damp but soon dry and dirty sponge. Importers may do little to correct this situation. If the pet store is one of many who think providing cricket gel or wet sponge is the proper way to offer water or that a dry substrate like sand is appropriate, the tarantula is left to rehydrate solely from its food. If the tarantula is not feeding, it may be doomed. Signs of dehydration include a shrunken, wrinkled, or misshapen abdomen and curled legs.

Obviously the best way to prevent dehydration is to always provide a source of fresh water, offer well-fed and watered prey items regularly, and maintain adequate moisture and humidity in the enclosure. Similarly, providing the same proper conditions will usually rehydrate a new acquisition. But what if you accidentally let an enclosure dry out or a tarantula ceases feeding and begins to show signs of dehydration? You must immediately try to rehydrate the spider, and this is done using what has become known in tarantulaculture as the ICU technique. The ICU is named after the intensive care unit found in human hospitals. It is a warm and moist chamber with greatly elevated humidity that keeps the tarantula in constant contact with moisture.

Creating an ICU is simple. First take a small opaque container like those sour cream and cottage cheese are sold in and clean it thoroughly. Use a larger or smaller container as necessary so that it isn't too much larger than the spider's leg span. Ventilate it slightly by adding three or four pinholes to the lid. Soak some paper toweling in 80°F (27°C) water and wad the towel in an inch (2.5 cm) or so deep substrate in

FAMILY-FRIENDLY TIP

Hands-Off Pets

Tarantulas are very fragile creatures that can be easily injured or killed by even the slightest fall. It is best to keep them as hands-off terrarium pets like tropical fish or tree frogs rather than subject even the most docile tarantula to risk from handling. Additionally, many popular species have defensive hairs that can cause severe irritation to the skin and mucous membranes. Children should be supervised when coming into contact with tarantulas or their cages and must wash their hands immediately afterward. Due both to the risk of injury to the tarantula and the hazard from the urticating hairs, children shouldn't handle tarantulas.

Tarantulas

Wild-caught tarantulas—especially rainforest species like the Goliath Bird-Eater—often suffer from dehydration.

the bottom of the container. Add more water as needed so that the towel is saturated and standing water rises just above its surface.

You must always be careful when using an ICU, as a tarantula will drown if it cannot keep its lung slits above water. If the tarantula is severely dehydrated I will add a bit more water and tilt the cup to create a pool of water in the low side while the side tilted up higher has no standing water. This allows the tarantula to be placed so its mouth is in the water, while its opisthosoma and its book lung openings are above the water line. Place the tarantula in the cup, secure the lid, and place the ICU in a warm (75 to 80°F [24 to 27°C]), dark, and quiet location. Do not heat the cup or place it where temperatures exceed the low 80s (27° to 29°C).

Fungal Infections

A tarantula that is kept in stagnant, overly moist conditions—often the result of poor ventilation—may develop fungus on its body. Whether the tarantula actually has a fungal infection or the fungus has just found a suitable surface on which to live can be debated, but it still indicates a husbandry problem. You must immediately correct the environmental conditions and provide a period of almost complete cage dryness. Maintaining very dry conditions with clean dry substrate for a week or two can help reduce or eliminate the fungus. During this time it is very important to monitor the tarantula several times a day to watch for dehydration. You can leave a very small water dish overnight a couple of times a week to minimize the risk

Common Pink-Toe suffering from a fungal infection. Fungal infections are usually caused by overly moist, stagnant conditions.

shaving cuts and the like. Petroleum jelly may be used in a pinch, but the use of a super glue or liquid bandage is increasingly popular. A cotton swab may be used to dab the chosen substance on the affected area.

A rupture of the body itself, whether the prosoma or opisthosoma, is a serious problem that usually results in death. Prompt application of super glue may be the tarantula's only hope. This may not save it, but it is better to make any attempt to save the spider than to give up completely.

Molting Problems

The molting process is when the tarantula is at greatest risk. Once ecdysis begins, the tarantula must complete its transformation or die. A tarantula that is housed correctly within an appropriate range of humidity and temperature will usually have no difficulty molting. A slight increase in humidity is beneficial and recommended during the molting period, but a healthy, well-nourished tarantula should be sufficiently hydrated to molt with ease.

One reason a tarantula might have difficulty extricating itself from its old

of desiccation. Some keepers have used antifungal powders, such as the horticultural fungicide Captan and those made for treating athlete's foot infections. These are applied carefully using a cotton swab, but this procedure must be recognized as experimental.

Injuries

The tarantula is encased in a protective exoskeleton, but it is still a fragile creature that can be wounded quite easily. The most common injury is a slight rupture of its body, most often caused by a fall or rough handling. Legs are the most common location for an injury that leaks hemolymph. Minor wounds will clot themselves, but treatment may be required if hemolymph continues to seep out. Corn starch and styptic powder can be used just as they are used to clot skin is old age. A tarantula's physical condition is critical to molting success, and an elderly specimen may be too weak to complete the process. In fact, it is during the molt that many old pet tarantulas die.

A common cause of molting problems is previous injury. For example, if a leg is damaged but not lost by autotomy (self-amputation), it may be difficult for the tarantula to extract it as it molts. That is why it is best to carefully amputate a severely injured leg at the coxa (the leg segment closest to the body). (*Note: This procedure may fatally injure the tarantula and should be attempted only by experienced keepers who accept the risk.*) Tarantulas that have difficulty extricating an injured limb during ecdysis may cast off the trapped leg during the molting process. This is the best possible situation, as the leg will regenerate with the following molt.

A tarantula should completely shed its skin within hours. A spider that has made no progress after eight hours may be hopelessly trapped. There is little the novice keeper can do. Humidity and warmth can be slightly increased and the enclosure covered so that the spider is in total darkness. The tarantula should be left completely undisturbed. It may be difficult to resist the temptation to check its status, but all the keeper can do is be patient. Sadly, the spider may have little hope.

Parasites

Parasitism is a relationship between organisms of different species by which one organism, known as the parasite,

I'm Not Dead! I'm Molting!

Sadly, many tarantulas are killed or discarded because their owners were not aware of the molting process. These keepers did not take the time to learn much about their pets and were surprised when they first encountered a tarantula that had flipped itself "belly up."

Dead tarantulas remain upright, usually with their legs curled beneath them. A tarantula that is lying upside down is about to molt and should be left undisturbed. Unaware keepers will sometimes flip the tarantula back over, thinking that they are helping when they are actually putting the vulnerable molting spider at great risk. After some frantic research to investigate the imagined problem, these keepers often learn that the tarantula was actually about to shed its exuvium, so they wonder whether they should correct their error by turning the spider over again. The answer is no. The damage is done and should not be compounded by again disturbing the spider while it is in its most delicate state. With any fortune, the tarantula will successfully shed its skin despite the intrusion. All that can be done is wait and hope.

benefits at the expense of the other, called the host. There are endoparasites that live within the body of their hosts, and ectoparasites that live outside their hosts. Parasites can affect most living things, including tarantulas.

Nematodes

Nematodes as a group include harmful parasitic roundworms that will devour a tarantula from the inside. They have increasingly become a problem in the tarantula hobby and are thought to originate with wild-caught tarantulas, particularly Asian species. They spread through a collection and may affect even healthy captive-bred spiders. Because parasitic nematodes spread very easily and infection is fatal, keepers must be diligent in eradicating infected spiders, either by quarantining them far away from other tarantulas or,

more effectively, by euthanizing them and removing the threat altogether.

Both feeder crickets and phorid flies, common pests, have been implicated as possible vectors that pass nematodes from host to new victim but, regardless of the vehicle that causes this affliction to spread, it is a serious problem that keepers must watch for. Signs of nematode infestation in tarantulas include:

- tarantula attacks prey but has great difficulty grasping it with the chelicerae
- pedipalps and front legs that seem paralyzed and are drawn unnaturally toward the body
- fluid leaking from the anus
- a foamy yellowish-white mass around the mouth area (this is composed of thousands of tiny worms)

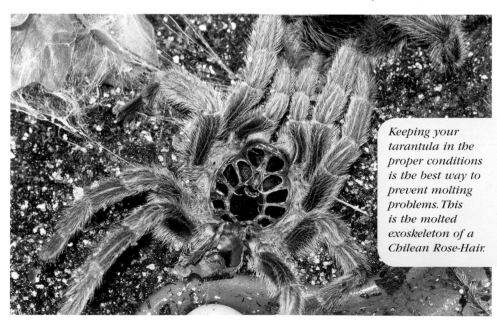

Keeping your tarantula in the proper conditions is the best way to prevent molting problems. This is the molted exoskeleton of a Chilean Rose-Hair.

Household Dangers for Tarantulas

The following items are deadly to tarantulas, and keepers must keep them away from their spiders:

- Fumes from bleach or ammonia
- Insecticides of any kind, including roach sprays and flea treatments for dogs and cats
- Fumes from overheated non-stick (Teflon) pans
- Mothballs
- Perfumes and air fresheners
- Solvents such as nail polish remover and paint thinner
- Tobacco smoke

Immediately isolate any spider suspected of nematode infection. If it refuses a meal, make sure you discard the uneaten prey rather than offering it to another tarantula (this is a good practice with all tarantulas). If the tarantula shows definite signs of nematodes, especially the curled and seemingly paralyzed forelegs and pedipalps and the obvious white foam surrounding the mouth, it should be euthanized.

Other Parasites

The most well-known tarantula parasite is one that doesn't affect captive tarantulas. This is the larvae of *Pepsis* and *Hemipepsis* wasps, which are commonly referred to as tarantula hawks. The wasp immobilizes a tarantula with its sting and then lays a single egg on the spider's body. Upon hatching, the emerging larva will feed on the still-living tarantula.

Mites are tiny organisms that, along with ticks, form a subclass of arachnids, making them distant relatives of the tarantula. Some are parasitic and some are not. Mites are occasionally seen on tarantulas or in tarantula enclosures, but it is unclear whether these are parasites of tarantulas. However, they can easily kill a tarantula by congregating around the soft tissue of the book lungs. Some live on the crickets we use as food for our spiders.

As with other unwelcome intruders, the potential for a mite problem can be greatly reduced with good enclosure sanitation, such as removing uneaten food and prey remains and avoiding overly damp conditions. Still, mites are so minute and require only the tiniest bits of food and moisture that even the cleanest of cages may continue to harbor them.

Methods of eradicating them include a complete stripping and cleaning of the cage, including replacing all substrate and décor and disinfecting the enclosure with a 5 percent bleach solution. Always rinse the enclosure extremely well after using dilute chlorine bleach. Alternatively, a tarantula can be housed in a temporary container for a few days while its entire enclosure is placed in a freezer in an attempt to kill all mites.

Pests

The most common pest of captive tarantulas is the phorid fly, also called scuttle fly. These humpbacked grayish flies are about the size of a fruit fly and are scavengers that are attracted to anything dead. Because crickets have extremely short life spans and high mortality, the phorid fly is commonly associated with domestic cricket farming. Keepers may never be able to completely prevent these flies, but their occurrence can be greatly reduced by maintaining excellent enclosure sanitation, especially prompt removal of food remains. A decaying cricket left in a tarantula cage is a phorid fly attractant. One of the reasons to avoid using pinkie mice and other vertebrate food for tarantulas is that they take too long for the spider to ingest, and the rotting prey item is like a welcome sign to the scavenging phorid fly.

A method that works well to reduce phorid fly populations is to use a bait trap. This is a container with a small hole that is filled with nasty decaying matter like a bunch of rotting crickets or a piece of raw meat. This provides an attractive target for the phorid flies, which find their way into the jar but cannot easily find their way back out. They will feed on the bait and lay eggs. The container can be left overnight and then placed directly into a freezer for a few days to kill the flies. This bait trap can be reused several times, and it becomes even more effective as it ages. It is not pleasant, but it works.

Starvation

A shriveled or sunken abdomen is typically a sign of extreme dehydration, not starvation, but occasionally a tarantula will refuse food for so long that its abdomen will become very small. Others fast for long periods with no apparent ill effects. This is especially true of the pet trade's ubiquitous and notorious problem feeder, the Chilean Rose-Hair. A tarantula that noticeably loses abdominal weight and is refusing food should be stimulated with a slight increase in both temperature and humidity. Keep the tarantula as dark as possible and disturb it only as necessary.

Offer small meals, such as a single cricket, every other night; remove the prey the following morning if not eaten. If the spider still refuses food, try a different prey item such as a superworm once or twice. If the tarantula still ignores all meals, place a cricket that has been slightly crushed to expose its moist insides in contact with the tarantula and leave it overnight.

The abdomen of this tarantula is horribly shrunken, a sure sign of starvation.

Remarkably enough, a tarantula that has refused to make its own kill may scavenge on this unsavory treat.

Euthanasia

There may come a time when a tarantula with no hope for recovery needs to be euthanized. Since tarantulas are *ectothermic*, dependent on their surroundings for body temperature, they can be chilled for a period of time and then frozen. First place the tarantula in a cup located in a refrigerator for a day or so to slow its body functions to a dormant state, and then transfer the cup to the freezer for 24 hours before disposal. Tarantulas may or may not feel anything like pain, but the refrigeration prior to freezing ensures that euthanasia is conducted as humanely as possible.

The Expert Knows

Fasting

One of the greatest concerns of new tarantula owners is their new spider's refusing to eat. This is rarely a cause for alarm. As long as an otherwise healthy tarantula is provided with the correct temperature and humidity range and access to fresh water, adult tarantulas can go many months without feeding. In fact, a period of dormancy or fasting may be part of some species' natural seasonal cycle. This phenomenon certainly seems to be why the common Chilean Rose-Hair frustrates so many keepers with its extended refusal of food.

Of course, tarantulas also do not feed prior to a molt, and young growing tarantulas that may molt as often as every couple of months will frequently have periods of weeks when they do not accept prey. If your tarantula doesn't eat, do not worry. Offer food at night and ensure that any uneaten prey is immediately removed in the morning. Try again in a week or two; if the tarantula still shows no interest, again remove the food promptly. Keep fresh water available and moisten the substrate slightly to elevate humidity. If the tarantula does molt, wait about one week for the tarantula's new skin to harden before offering food.

If a tarantula continues to refuse to eat even though a molt does not appear to be imminent, you can try increasing the enclosure temperature by a few degrees and lightly misting the cage (not the spider) with warm water once or twice a day. This increase in warmth and humidity will often stimulate the reluctant tarantula to resume feeding.

Chapter 4

Featured Species

This chapter showcases 20 popular pet tarantulas. Previously I've made brief mention of some of the best beginner species, and many of those are covered in greater detail here. Additionally, this chapter covers some admired species that are perhaps more suited to the experienced tarantulaculturist.

Quick Reference Guide to the Featured Species

Scientific Name	Common Name	Range	Experience Level*
Acanthoscurria geniculata	Brazilian Giant White-Knee	Brazil	Intermediate
Aphonopelma seemanni	Stripe-Knee	Central America	Novice
Avicularia versicolor	Antilles Pink-Toe	Lesser Antilles	Novice
Brachypelma smithi	Mexican Red-Knee	Pacific coast of central Mexico	Novice
Ceratogyrus darlingi	Straight-Horned Baboon	Southern Africa	Intermediate
Chilobrachys fimbriatus	Indian Violet	India	Intermediate
Chromatopelma cyaneopubescens	Greenbottle Blue	Northern Venezuela	Novice
Ephebopus murinus	Skeleton	French Guiana	Intermediate
Eucratoscelus pachypus	Stout-Leg Baboon	Tanzania	Novice
Grammostola porteri	Chilean Rose-Hair	Chile	Novice
Grammostola pulchra	Brazilian Black	Brazil and Uruguay	Novice
Haplopelma lividum	Cobalt Blue	Myanmar and Thailand	Advanced
Heteroscodra maculata	Ornamental Baboon	West Africa	Intermediate/ Advanced
Hysterocrates gigas	Cameroon Baboon	West-central Africa	Intermediate
Lasiodora parahybana	Brazilian Salmon-Pink	Brazil	Intermediate
Megaphobema mesomelas	Costa Rican Red-Leg	Costa Rica	Intermediate
Pelinobius muticus	King Baboon	Eastern Africa	Advanced
Poecilotheria regalis	Indian Ornamental	India	Intermediate/ Advanced
Psalmopoeus irminia	Venezuelan Suntiger	Venezuela	Intermediate/ Advanced
Theraphosa blondi	Goliath Bird-Eater	Brazil, Guyana, Venezuela	Advanced

*The three experience levels used here—novice, intermediate, and advanced—are obviously subjective distinctions. In fact, a conscientious novice keeper might have no difficulty keeping an advanced species. For some insight into why each experience level was chosen, please refer to the comments in the species profiles.

Acanthoscurria geniculata, Brazilian Giant White-Knee

Habitat: a terrestrial species found in the forests of Brazil
Adult Leg Span: 6-8 inches (15-20 cm)
Captive Diet: crickets, roaches, superworms and other large insects, nightcrawlers
Temperature: 75°-80°F (24°-27°C)
Humidity: 60-75%
Growth Rate: moderately fast
Comments: This species is very common in the hobby, partly because females produce a huge number of tiny spiderlings and these young tarantulas grow fairly rapidly. It is a very attractive species with striking white leg markings and a reddish abdomen. It has a strong tendency to flick its very powerful urticating hairs. It is fairly nervous and defensive, but it is not overly aggressive. It has a strong feeding response and will tackle large prey. Care should be taken to ensure that large adults are not overfed. It is fairly active and makes an excellent display tarantula.

The Brazilian Giant-White Knee is a beautiful but fairly nervous tarantula.

Similar Species: A number of other *Acanthoscurria* are popular in the hobby, including the extremely similar *A. brocklehursti* and the smaller, calmer, and more drably colored Bolivian Salmon (*A. chacoana*) and Chaco Mousy Brown (*A. insubtilis*).

Aphonopelma seemanni, Stripe-Knee/Costa Rican Zebra

Habitat: a burrowing species found in the grasslands and forests of Central America
Adult Leg Span: 4.5-5.5 inches (11.4-14 cm)
Captive Diet: crickets and other insects
Temperature: 74°-78°F (23°-26°C)
Humidity: 60-70%
Growth Rate: moderate
Comments: The wide-ranging genus *Aphonopelma* includes the spiders of the American Southwest, which are plainly colored but hardy and easy to keep. The most popular member of the genus is a much more attractive Central American species known as the Stripe-Knee. It is also often called the Costa Rican Zebra, but it actually ranges throughout much of Central America. Paler specimens come from the northern end of the range and are available as imported wild-caught spiders. The darker, more attractively colored "true Costa Rican" form is only available as captive-bred animals because Costa Rica does not export wildlife. The Stripe-Knee is a bit nervous, but many specimens are quite docile. It does not have a tremendous appetite and will feed sparingly on crickets.

The Stripe-Knee is an excellent choice for first-time keepers.

Similar Species: *A. seemanni* is one of the southernmost representatives of a wide-ranging genus that includes the American tarantulas. Another popular species is the Mexican Blood-Leg (*A. bicoloratum*). All *Aphonopelma* are

obligate burrowers that are suited to the novice keeper.

Avicularia versicolor, Antilles Pink-Toe/Martinique Tree Spider

Habitat: an arboreal species found in the tropical forests of Martinique and Guadeloupe (Lesser Antilles)
Adult Leg Span: 3.5-5 inches (9-13 cm)
Captive Diet: crickets, moths, flies, and other insects; the wild diet includes lizards and tree frogs, and some breeders supplement with these prey items
Temperature: 75°-80°F (24°-27°C)
Humidity: 70-80%
Growth Rate: fast
Comments: The Martinique Tree Spider is among the most beautiful tarantulas in the world. It starts life as an electric-

Native Species in the Hobby

The genus *Aphonopelma* contains many species that are easy for hobbyists to keep and have fairly calm dispositions. This wide-ranging genus is well represented in the American Southwest, and many species are available to the tarantulaculturist. Two favorites are the Mexican Blonde (*A. chalcodes*), which is found from Arizona south to Mexico, and the Texas or Oklahoma Brown (*A. hentzi*), which ranges from Kansas south to Texas and northern Mexico.

Mexican Blonde (left) and Texas Brown tarantulas (right).

The Metallic Tree Spider is a large, docile, and popular pink-toe.

blue spiderling that gradually becomes a dazzling purplish, magenta, or reddish-pink tarantula with a green carapace. This species can be a bit difficult for beginners to keep due to the delicate balance required between excellent ventilation and sufficient humidity. These tropical tarantulas require moisture, but stagnant conditions will quickly kill them. Those willing to put in the effort to maintain suitable conditions are rewarded with a fascinating spider that does well in a naturalistic terrarium.

Similar Species: All of the "avics" or pink-toed tarantulas build tubular silk retreats and have interesting habits. The Common Pink-Toe (*Avicularia avicularia*) is imported for the pet trade, and wild-caught adults are often found in pet stores. Some may adapt to captivity well, but many are in poor condition or are mature males that will soon perish. The keeper interested in these pink-toed tree spiders will find rearing young and colorful spiderlings

of *A. versicolor* or the Purple Tree Spider (*A. purpurea*) much more rewarding. The large and docile White-Toe or Metallic Tree Spider (*A. metallica*) is another similar species that is captive bred for the pet trade.

Brachypelma smithi, Mexican Red-Knee

Habitat: a burrowing species found in the scrub forest of the Pacific coast of central Mexico (Colima and Guerrero states)
Adult Leg Span: 5-6 inches (13-15 cm)
Captive Diet: crickets and other insects
Temperature: 72°-76°F (22°-25°C)
Humidity: 50-70%
Growth Rate: slow
Comments: The Mexican Red-Knee has been the classic pet tarantula for over 30 years, and there is good reason for that. It is a gorgeous tarantula with a dark body and striking orange markings

Wild Mexican Red-Knees are protected by law, but this tarantula is captive bred in large numbers.

on its legs. It is also docile and very easy to care for. It is one of the most popular first tarantulas. Now protected in the wild, the genus *Brachypelma* is well established in the hobby, with captive-bred animals readily available. Spiderlings grow somewhat slowly, with captive males maturing in six or seven years and females at about ten. A female can live in excess of 30 years, making it a sort of heirloom pet. The most significant problem with these tarantulas is their penchant for "flicking hairs," or rubbing the urticating bristles off their abdomens in defense. People vary in their sensitivity to this irritant, but it is something to keep in mind.

Defensive or Aggressive

With the spectacular defensive displays of some tarantulas, such as the Cobalt Blue and Venezuelan Suntiger, it is tempting to refer to these seemingly ferocious species as aggressive. The truth is that, like most other animals, all tarantulas would rather flee than fight. When disturbed, they may be left with no choice than to defend themselves aggressively, but this doesn't mean that the act is one of aggression. For tarantulas such as the two mentioned here and others with a menacing threat display—such as a reared-back and stridulating King Baboon—the term "highly defensive" is much more appropriate than "aggressive."

Similar Species: All of the red-legs from the Pacific coast of Mexico are colorful, hardy, and usually quite docile. Other popular *Brachypelma* are the Mexican Fire-Leg (*B. boehmei*) and the Mexican Painted Red-Leg (*B. emilia*). The Honduran Curly-Hair (*B. albopilosum*) is another hardy and recommended species.

Ceratogyrus darlingi, Straight-Horned Baboon

Habitat: a burrowing species found in the grasslands of southern Africa
Adult Leg Span: 5 inches (12.7 cm)
Captive Diet: crickets and other insects
Temperature: 72°-76°F (22° 25°C)
Humidity: 65-75%
Growth Rate: moderate
Comments: The tarantulas of this genus are referred to as horned baboons because they have a horn-like projection called the foveal protuberance rising from the center of the carapace. In this species it is straight, with a slight curve to the rear. These spiders are active terrarium subjects that will construct intricate burrows and silk tubes. Also interesting are their hammock-style egg sacs, which differ from the typical spherical sac of most tarantulas.

They are highly defensive tarantulas and, despite the relative ease of caring for them in captivity, are best left to more experienced keepers. Although the horned baboons inhabit relatively dry areas, they are deep burrowers that do not fare well in overly dry cages. Until recently this spider was known as *Ceratogyrus bechuanicus*.

Straight-Horned Baboons are interesting tarantulas, but they are fast and defensive spiders best suited for experienced keepers.

Similar Species: Several other species of horned baboon tarantulas are found in the hobby, although determining which is which is complicated by changes in taxonomy. The Unicorn Baboon (*C. marshalli*) has a particularly impressive vertical foveal horn that gives it its common name.

Chilobrachys fimbriatus, Indian Violet

Habitat: a burrowing species found in the dry and the moist forests of the Western Ghats of coastal western India
Adult Leg Span: 4 inches (10 cm)
Captive Diet: crickets and other insects
Temperature: 74°-78°F (23°-26°C)
Humidity: 60-70%
Growth Rate: moderately fast
Comments: The Indian Violet is a beautifully marked spider with a metallic purplish or burgundy coloration and a banded abdomen. Tarantulas of the genus *Chilobrachys* dig deep

burrows and fill their terrariums with an abundance of silk using their long spinnerets to great effect. The Indian Violet is highly defensive and very fast. It is much smaller than other *Chilobrachys,* with adult females rarely exceeding 4 inches (10.2 cm) and many males maturing at about 2 inches (5 cm) in leg span. In fact, ultimate males are much smaller than females in many Asian tarantulas, and the difference may be most dramatic in this genus.
Similar Species: There are one or two other *Chilobrachys* that are common in the pet trade, but identifying them to the correct species level is difficult. The most frequently seen name is *C. huahini,* but this may be inaccurate. They are unmarked brownish tarantulas that are much larger than *C. fimbriatus.*

Chromatopelma cyaneopubescens, Greenbottle Blue

Habitat: a terrestrial species found in the desert scrub of northern Venezuela's Paraguana Peninsula
Adult Leg Span: 4-5 inches (10-13 cm)
Captive Diet: crickets and other insects
Temperature: 72°-78°F (22°-26°C)
Humidity: 40-50%
Growth Rate: fast
Comments: This incredibly colorful tarantula makes an excellent display animal. Adults are gaudy spiders with bright blue legs, an orange abdomen, and green carapace. They tend to stay out in the open and create fascinating silk structures in the terrarium. It is a bit too fast and nervous to be considered docile in the sense of most *Grammostola* or *Brachypelma,* but it is

The brilliantly colored Greenbottle Blue is a hardy tarantula with a big appetite.

not overly defensive. Because it is also hardy and easy to care for it makes an excellent beginner species for those who prefer a hands-off terrarium pet. It inhabits a very harsh, dry climate and, as a result, is extremely hardy in captivity. Keep its cage mostly dry and provide plenty of ventilation. The Greenbottle Blue or "GBB" has a voracious appetite, and young spiders will take food as big as themselves and grow rapidly.
Similar Species: None

Ephebopus murinus, Skeleton Tarantula

Habitat: a burrowing species (semi-arboreal when young) found in the lowland tropical forests of northern South America
Adult Leg Span: 4-5 inches (10-13 cm)
Captive Diet: crickets and other insects

Temperature: 75°-80°F (24-27°C)
Humidity: 70-80%
Growth Rate: moderate
Comments: The Skeleton bears a superficial resemblance to the Stripe-Knee (*Aphonopelma seemanni*), but they have little in common. Whereas the latter is a fairly placid species that is an excellent choice for beginners, the Skeleton Tarantula is a highly defensive spider that becomes agitated at the slightest disturbance. The genus *Ephebopus* is unique in two ways. Spiderlings and juveniles are primarily arboreal before becoming burrowing adults (it is closely related to the tarantulas of the arboreal genus *Avicularia*), and this is the only genus that has urticating bristles on its pedipalps and can flick hairs from the front of its body.

The Expert Knows

Measuring Tarantulas

There are two methods used to measure tarantula size. Outside the United States, tarantula measurements are generally total body lengths. That is, the combined lengths of the prosoma and opisthosoma including the chelicerae. This is the most precise form of measurement, but it does not give the full impression of a tarantula's size. US keepers use the tarantula's leg span, which is accurately measured diagonally from the tip of Leg I (front) on one side of the body to the tip of Leg IV (rear) on the opposite side. The result is a measurement that takes into account both body size and leg length.

Similar Species: The most sought-after member of the genus is the Blue Fang (*E. cyanognathus*). This common name is inaccurate, because it is the chelicerae or jaws that are brilliant blue, not the actual fangs. It is a very attractive tarantula, with a greenish-gold abdomen and reddish-brown legs with a yellow band between the femur and patella.

Eucratolscelus pachypus, Stout-Leg Baboon

Habitat: a burrowing species found in the scrubby grasslands of Tanzania (and probably Kenya)
Adult Leg Span: 4-5 inches (10-13 cm)
Captive Diet: crickets and other insects
Temperature: 74°-78°F (23°-26°C)
Humidity: 60-70%
Growth Rate: slow
Comments: This plain brown species is featured here because it is the best introduction to the Old World tarantulas. Unlike most other African tarantulas, it is calm and fairly docile. Because Old World tarantulas do not have urticating bristles, the Stout-Leg Baboon is a rare combination of placid temperament and lack of hair-flicking in a tarantula that is also very easy to keep. It gets its common name from its hind legs, which are much thicker than the rest of its legs. Unfortunately, confusion surrounds this spider, as many reptile importers incorrectly market this tarantula to pet stores as the Feather-Leg Baboon, a name that is more accurately applied to an arboreal West African species (*Stromatopelma calceatum*). The difference is

The Stout-Leg Baboon is one of the few Old World tarantulas suitable for novice keepers.

significant, as *Eucratoscelus* is a spider suitable for novice keepers and the pet trade, whereas *Stromatopelma* is among the fastest and most defensive tarantulas in the world and is thought to have a particularly toxic venom.
Similar Species: There is a second species of *Eucratoscelus* in Kenya (*E. constrictus*) that occasionally enters the hobby.

Grammostola porteri, Chilean Rose-Hair

Habitat: a burrowing species found in the grasslands of Chile
Adult Leg Span: 4-5 inches (10-13 cm)
Captive Diet: crickets and other insects
Temperature: 70°-76°F (21°-24°C)
Humidity: 60-70%
Growth Rate: slow
Comments: This is the most common tarantula in the pet trade, with a seemingly endless supply of wild-caught adults ending up in pet shops.

However, it is a problematic species that frustrates many new keepers and may discourage further exploration of the tarantula hobby. This species either never moves at all or never settles into its cage and constantly wanders. Some are very inactive for extended periods and then abruptly seem to become incessantly active. The wandering specimens are at great risk of injury, as they will often climb the sides of an aquarium and hang upside down from the top, where they might fall. The aspect of Chilean Rose-Hair behavior that is even more disconcerting to new keepers is that it often fasts for a considerable amount of time. It is likely the Chilean Rose-Hair goes through a natural feeding cycle in the wild in which it does not eat for months when weather conditions are harsh and/or the food is scarce. In truth, this is common among many wild animals, and eating once a week on a normal routine (as in captivity) certainly isn't a natural occurrence. If your tarantula is well fed and has access to fresh water, it can easily go for months without eating. Offer food every couple of weeks and if it is refused remove it immediately. Wait another couple of weeks, or even a month, and try again.

Similar Species: The Chilean Rose-Hair has been known by many scientific names, including *Grammostola rosea*, *G. spatulata (spathulata),* and *G. cala*. Now referred to as *G. porteri*, there is confusion among hobbyists regarding whether these different names have referred to different spiders or color forms of the same spider. Tarantula keepers have long thought that there are at least two species of Chilean Rose-Hair—the brownish spider that is somewhat rose-pink after a molt and is the common pet trade spider we now call *G. porteri*, and the much more reddish-pink form that has been often called *G. cala* and may now be called *G. rosea*.

Grammostola pulchra, Brazilian Black

Habitat: a burrowing species found in the grasslands of Uruguay and Brazil
Adult Leg Span: 5-6 inches (13-15 cm)
Captive Diet: crickets and other insects
Temperature: 72°-77°F (22°-25°C)
Humidity: 60-70%
Growth Rate: slow
Comments: This species certainly ranks among the best pet tarantulas. I like to refer to the Brazilian Black as the "black Labrador Retriever" of the tarantula hobby because these

Unfortunately, few breeders produce Chilean Rose-Hairs; almost all of them are wild caught.

The Brazilian Black is a large, docile, and hardy spider. What more could a tarantula keeper want?

tarantulas are big, black, and gentle like the dog. It is highly recommended for novice keepers and is one of the most sought-after tarantulas in the hobby. This species has proved problematic to breed in captivity. This difficulty in breeding in captivity is no doubt related to seasonal cycles that in nature cause a period of dormancy. Like its genus-mate (congeneric) the Chilean Rose-Hair, it may fast for several months when conditions would be unfavorable in its natural habitat. The greatest success in breeding this species has come from an artificial hibernation period brought on by keeping it at very cool temperatures for a couple of months.

Similar Species: The Chaco Gold-Knee or Gold-Striped (*Grammostola pulchripes*) is a very similar, albeit more colorful, tarantula. It is the Golden Retriever to *G. pulchra*'s Black Lab. Along with the Pink Zebra Beauty (*Eupalaestrus campestratus*), which is similar in care, habits, and temperament, *G. pulchra* and *G. pulchripes* are the best pet tarantulas you will find.

The genus Grammostola *has a number of species that are excellent terrarium pets, including* G. pulchripes *(left) and* G. iheringi *(right).*

Haplopelma lividum, Cobalt Blue

Habitat: a burrowing species found in the rainforests of Burma and Thailand
Adult Leg Span: 4-5 inches (10-13 cm)
Captive Diet: crickets and other insects, earthworms
Temperature: 75°-78°F (24°-26°C)
Humidity: 70-80%
Growth Rate: moderate
Comments: This black and blue tarantula has plenty of attitude. Commonly imported for the pet trade, it is often purchased by those who find its electric blue coloration or highly defensive demeanor appealing. However, a properly housed Cobalt Blue will never be seen, and the vivid coloration of a freshly molted specimen will go unappreciated. This is a species that lives in burrows in humid forests, and it will thrive in captivity only if it is allowed to dig tunnels and secrete itself far below the surface. Keepers who specialize in this spider and other Asian burrowing tarantulas use tall enclosures that are filled with 10 inches (25.4 cm) or more of damp soil. Many keepers make a starter burrow with a broom handle or similar dowel, but a tarantula will soon dig its way deep into the substrate even without this head start. **Similar Species:** The Thai Zebra (*Haplopelma albostriatum*) and Thai Black or Thai Orange-Fringed (*Ornithoctonus aureotibialis*) require the same captive care, especially the need to burrow in damp soil, and also share the Cobalt Blue's spirited disposition.

Keepers must provide the Cobalt Blue and its relatives with deep humid burrows.

Heteroscodra maculata, Ornamental Baboon/Togo Starburst

Habitat: an arboreal species found in palms and bushes of the forests of western Africa
Adult Leg Span: 4-5 inches (10-13 cm)
Captive Diet: crickets and other insects
Temperature: 75°-78°F (24°-26°C)
Humidity: 70-80%
Growth Rate: moderately fast
Comments: This pale gray, tan, and white tree tarantula has a ghostly appearance and nervous temperament. Wild-caught adults are often available in the pet trade, but captive-bred spiderlings are easy to acquire, as the captive care and breeding of *H. maculata* is quite straightforward. It is very shy and secretive, and many specimens will ignore the heights of their terrarium and favor a retreat created closer to the ground. In fact, spiderlings have a strong tendency to burrow.

Although the Ornamental Baboon is an arboreal species, it will sometimes burrow in the terrarium.

Similar Species: This tarantula's common name is borrowed from the "true" ornamental tarantulas of India and Sri Lanka, but this African arboreal is not related. Its closest cousin is the Feather-Leg Baboon (*Stromatopelma calceatum*), which also lives above the ground in western Africa.

Hysterocrates gigas, Cameroon Baboon

Habitat: a burrowing species found in the forests of west-central Africa
Adult Leg Span: 6-8 inches (15-20 cm)
Captive Diet: crickets and other insects
Temperature: 75°-80°F (24-27°C)
Humidity: 70-80%
Growth Rate: moderately fast
Comments: This large velvety brown

baboon tarantula is very popular due to its size and aggressive appetite. One of the most fascinating aspects of its biology is that a couple of generations of offspring may live together in the wild, sharing a retreat with their mother. This social behavior allows for captive-bred spiderlings to be raised communally.

Similar Species: The taxonomy of this tarantula has always confused keepers. Some believe that two or three different species of *Hysterocrates* are found in the hobby, whereas others would argue that it is one species misidentified. The greatest debate surrounds the species *H. hercules*, which is among the largest tarantulas in the world. Tales told by long-time hobbyists regarding the time they had "true hercules" are probably misguided, as it is unlikely that this species has ever found its way into the tarantula hobby.

The Cameroon Baboon is one of the few tarantulas that live communally in nature.

The Brazilian Salmon-Pink has become common in the pet trade because females may lay 2,000 eggs at a time.

Lasiodora parahybana, Brazilian Salmon-Pink

Habitat: a terrestrial species found in the forests of Brazil
Adult Leg Span: 7-10 inches or more (18-25 cm)
Captive Diet: roaches and other large insects, small vertebrates
Temperature: 74°-78°F (23°-26°C)
Humidity: 60-70%
Growth Rate: moderately fast
Comments: The Brazilian Salmon-Pink (or Salmon-Pink Bird-Eater) is a brown spider with pinkish bristles. This enormous tarantula rivals the Goliath Bird-Eater in size but makes a much better terrarium tarantula. Not prone to seclude itself in a retreat, it makes for an excellent display animal. The Brazilian Salmon-Pink is a somewhat defensive and imposing tarantula with powerful urticating bristles, but it is typically much calmer than the Goliath. But what truly makes it a

better choice for those who want a giant tarantula is that it is inexpensive and easy to care for. *L. parahybana* egg sacs may contain more than 2000 tiny spiderlings, making this spider readily available to hobbyists looking for a huge showcase tarantula. It grows quickly and has an insatiable appetite.
Similar Species: A closely related species with more reddish rather than pinkish hairs, *L. difficilis* (Brazilian Fiery Red) is also often found in the hobby.

Megaphobema mesomelas, Costa Rican Red-Leg

Habitat: a burrowing species found in the mountain forests of Costa Rica
Adult Leg Span: 5-6 inches (13-15 cm)
Captive Diet: nightcrawlers, crickets, and other insects
Temperature: 70°-76°F (21°-24°C)
Humidity: 70-80%
Growth Rate: moderate
Comments: This gorgeous tarantula inhabits the montane cloud forests of Costa Rica. It is a striking velvety

Female Costa Rican Red-Leg tending her egg sac.

black with bright orange on its legs. It feeds on a host of arthropods, but also consumes the large worms that share the moist soil of its roadbank and forest floor burrows. It is somewhat rare in captivity, but it does quite well if kept cool (room temperature) and humid and provided with deep, moist substrate. Those keepers who are fortunate enough to add this species to their collections are rewarded with one of the tarantula world's true beauties. **Similar Species:** The Colombian Giant (*M. robustum*) is more readily available, but, while attractive in its own right, it is a far more nervous tarantula prone to flicking hairs.

Pelinobius muticus, King Baboon

Habitat: a burrowing species found in the scrubland of eastern Africa
Adult Leg Span: 6-8 inches (15-20 cm)
Captive Diet: roaches and other large insects
Temperature: 75°-80°F (24-27°C)
Humidity: 65-75%
Growth Rate: slow
Comments: This extremely defensive species is among the largest of Old World tarantulas, and with its stout legs and impressive hissing display it is a formidable spider. When disturbed it assumes a defensive threat posture by rearing up on its back legs and producing a hissing or buzzing sound by stridulation (rubbing specialized bristles on the chelicerae and pedipalps together). Although it has no pattern, the King Baboon's velvety reddish-brown coloration makes it

When threatened, the King Baboon produces a hissing sound by rubbing bristles on the pedipalps and chelicerae together.

a particularly handsome beast. It is a deep burrower that does best in captivity when provided with a considerable depth of slightly moist substrate. Unfortunately, this means the spider will seldom be seen, as it tunnels deep into its enclosure. Large specimens require fairly large food, and adult *Blaberus* roaches are ideal. Although the King Baboon will eagerly accept small vertebrates such as nestling rodents, the use of this food is problematic, as outlined in Chapter 2. Due to its size and temperament and reportedly fairly potent venom, the King Baboon is a tarantula recommended only for experienced keepers. Note that until very recently, this tarantula's scientific name was *Citharischius crawshayi.*
Similar Species: None.

Indian Ornamentals are less defensive than some of the other ornamental species.

Poecilotheria regalis, Indian Ornamental

Habitat: an arboreal species found in the forests of India
Adult Leg Span: 6-7 inches (15-18 cm)
Captive Diet: crickets, roaches, moths and other insects
Temperature: 75°-78°F (24°-25.6°C)
Humidity: 60-75%
Growth Rate: fast
Comments: The ornamental tarantulas of India and Sri Lanka, also known as tiger spiders, are among the most popular tarantulas in the terrarium. They are magnificent spiders with intricate coloration and pattern. The demand for these incredible spiders has fueled many successful captive breeding projects, and a number of species are readily available. None is more popular than the Indian Ornamental, and it is without a doubt the best introduction to the captive care of the tiger spiders. The blackish

legs of the Indian species are banded with white, and the forelegs have yellow coloration on the underside. The spider's defensive posture exposes these bright yellow patches. This flash of bright color serves to startle would-be attackers and warn of its bite. The dark abdomen has a pale foliate pattern above and a wide whitish band beneath.

Although novice keepers usually avoid the ornamental tarantulas because of their reputation for speed and aggression, they are actually somewhat shy spiders that will attempt to hide or flee when disturbed and stand their ground defensively only when there is no quick escape. Keepers of ornamental tarantulas recognize a spectrum of defensiveness from the fairly placid *P. metallica* and *P. miranda* to the more notably irascible *P. striata* and *P. ornata*, and *P. regalis* is in the middle of this range of temperaments, leaning somewhat toward the calmer side. Another reason that the tiger spiders are considered more for advanced keepers is the common belief that their venom is the most potent of all tarantula venoms. There are no studies to prove this, but anecdotal reports from those who have been bitten by tarantulas do confirm that envenomation from *Poecilotheria* bites seems to have the most serious effects. Severe pain, muscular cramps, and even coma-like symptoms have been reported.
Similar Species: Most of the 15 species of *Poecilotheria* are found in the hobby, with many being bred regularly,

Many species of ornamental tarantulas are captive bred and available to the tarantula hobbyist. Pictured here are (from top to bottom) the Gooty Sapphire, the Bengal Spotted (P. miranda), and the Fringed.

including the brilliant blue and yellow Gooty Sapphire (*P. metallica*), and the two largest species: the Fringed (*P. ornata*) and the Giant Redslate (*P. rufilata*). *P. rufilata* is a highland species and needs cooler temperatures and more moisture than the other *Poecilotheria*. The Kandy Highland (*P. subfusca*) and Yellow-Backed (*P. smithi*) Ornamentals are also highland species and should be treated accordingly.

Psalmopoeus irminia, Venezuelan Suntiger

Habitat: an arboreal species found in the tropical forests of Venezuela
Adult Leg Span: 5-6 inches (13-15 cm)
Captive Diet: crickets, moths, and other insects
Temperature: 75°-78°F (24°-26°C)
Humidity: 70-80%
Growth Rate: fast
Comments: The striking black and orange coloration of this spider makes it well suited to Halloween. Some would argue that its behavior is also reminiscent of scary monsters. This tarantula is so highly defensive that I would forgive the use of the term "aggressive" to describe its threat response, and I have actually used the word "psychotic" more than once to describe this easily agitated and

Featured Species

One of the fastest and most defensive tarantulas, the Venezuelan Suntiger is nevertheless popular with experienced keepers.

lightning-fast tree spider. This behavior certainly doesn't dissuade all keepers, and the Venezuelan Suntiger is a popular terrarium tarantula.
Similar Species: The olive-colored Trinidad Chevron (*P. cambridgei*) is another common representative of the genus in captivity. It is a larger

spider that may reach 7 inches (17.8 cm) or more and is sometimes seen in zoos and other public collections. Two smaller members of the genus, the Panamanian Blonde (*P. pulcher*) and the Costa Rican Orange-Mouth (*P. reduncus*), are also bred in captivity. All members of the genus typically have a rather irascible temperament.

Theraphosa blondi, Goliath Bird-Eater

Habitat: a burrowing species found in the forests of northern South America
Adult Leg Span: 8-10 inches or more (20-25 cm)
Captive Diet: large arthropods
Temperature: 77°-82°F (25°-28°C)
Humidity: 80-90%
Growth Rate: moderate
Comments: This tarantula is the world's largest spider. This alone makes it in great demand by tarantula keepers. However, keeping Goliath Bird-Eaters is not an easy task. The wild-caught adults that enter the pet trade each year are often in terrible shape. Many are gassed out of their burrows or subjected to improper, even horrible, conditions. This spider does not fare well without warmth and considerable moisture and humidity, and housing it within correct environmental parameters is a balancing act in an attempt to provide it moist, almost swampy, conditions with enough ventilation to prevent the air from becoming stagnant. Of course, captive-bred spiders do much better than imported adults, and with the size of *T. blondi* spiderlings (1 inch [2.5 cm] in leg span at 2nd instar!) they are very

The Goliath Bird-Eater has exacting requirements, which, combined with its large size, make it a tarantula only for experienced keepers.

popular with keepers. All prospective keepers of this species should be warned that the urticating bristles of the Goliath Bird-Eater have no rival for the irritation they can cause. Exposure to these airborne irritant hairs causes severe itching and, in some cases, respiratory distress.

Similar Species: The Pink-Foot Goliath (*T. apophysis*) has a leaner build and a slightly larger leg span. It gets its common name from the pinkish tarsi of young specimens, but it is its species name (*apophysis*) that is more interesting. While ultimate males of *T. blondi* do not have tibial apophyses or mating hooks, those of *T. apophysis* do. There is a new tarantula in the hobby that is referred to as the Burgundy Goliath that has characteristics of both previously described *Theraphosa* species but appears to be easier to keep and breed than either. It was recently given the name *T. stirmi*.

Chapter 5

Breeding Your

Tarantulas

Tarantula keepers are passionate about their hobby and soon discover that it is a very fascinating and addictive pursuit. With a rapidly growing collection and a thirst for knowledge, many tarantulaculturists eventually begin to consider captive breeding. Whether breeding is your goal or you just have an ultimate male that you want to have a chance at reproducing before its life cycle is complete, you may enter the exciting world of tarantula captive propagation. You don't have to be an expert to try breeding your pets. In fact, the tarantula hobby has been fueled by the captive breeding efforts of hobbyists just like you who made the transition from keeper to breeder. Here we present a brief overview of tarantula captive breeding.

Pairing up Your Spiders

The biggest challenge in tarantula captive breeding is having a sexually mature pair ready for mating at the same time. For a male, this means he must have recently had his ultimate molt. Previously lacking reproductive anatomy, this is his one chance to be fruitful and multiply. Females, by contrast, have a number of seasons of breeding in their lives. Once sexually mature, a female may mate and produce an egg sac each year until she is old. Some females may even produce two or more egg sacs in a season, at least in captivity where food is abundant and conditions are stable.

Still, the female isn't always ready for mating. There is one period within her molt cycle that is optimal for successful breeding. For the tarantula breeder, this usually means a female that molted one to several months earlier. After mating, females retain sperm in an organ called the spermatheca and produce an egg sac months down the road. The longer it has been since a molt, the greater chance she will molt after mating and, since she sheds the lining of her spermatheca with the rest of her exoskeleton, a molted female becomes infertile and must mate again.

For a tarantula keeper to have a mature pair in which both male and female are ready to mate simultaneously, he or she may have to raise quite a few specimens of the same species. In fact, it is usually

In many tarantulas, the female (right) is dramatically larger than the male (left) as seen in this pair of Kandy Highland Ornamentals.

Breeding Loan

The breeding loan is the great conduit for captive propagation and has been incredibly important in giving tarantulaculturists more than 100 species to enjoy. The premise is simple. A keeper with an ultimate male loans him to a fellow hobbyist who has a ready female. The two keepers may be friends or may have found each other through a tarantula society, reptile and exotic animal show, or Internet forum. The male may be exchanged locally or shipped across the country, but the female typically remains where she is. It is the responsibility of the owner of the female to mate the pair and, in the event of mating success, facilitate egg sac incubation.

Most breeding loans are 50-50 arrangements, with an equal share of any offspring that result. Normally the owner of the male is responsible for all freight charges necessary to get the male to the female or have a share of the spiderlings returned. Some keepers prefer to sell the male outright and forfeit any claim to breeding success, and others come to some other mutually acceptable deal. However the details are worked out, the joint venture to propagate tarantulas is to be applauded.

necessary to have a few age classes that include spiders that were hatched years apart. Males may mature long before females of the same age, especially in the slow-growing and long-lived species. But, more often than not, a keeper has either only a lone male or female of the species, or doesn't have a pair with both spiders ready for mating. For this keeper to become involved in captive breeding, he or she must network with other tarantula enthusiasts and form a partnership. Such a partnership often takes the form of a breeding loan (see sidebar: Breeding Loan).

Tarantula Reproduction

The rhythmic dance of the male and female tarantula rivals many of the great courtship displays found in the animal kingdom. Through messages tapped out by a flurry of drumming legs, a pair of tarantulas communicates mating intentions and receptiveness. When the female is responsive, the male becomes cautiously persistent and, with hopeful advances often accompanied by nervous retreats, seeks to engage his sperm-filled palpal bulbs with the female's epigynum and the spermathecae that lie within.

The Sperm Web

Before courtship can commence, the male must begin his ultimate journey. Having gone through the transition of his ultimate molt, the male has acquired his reproductive organs: the bulbs (emboli) at the end of his pedipalps. In some species, the males also grow tibial hooks (apophyses) that will aid in lifting the female and keeping him a safe distance from her jaws. Before setting out on his journey to find a mate, the male must load his bulbs with sperm.

The mature male constructs a sperm web using silk produced from his epiandrous glands. The construction varies with species, but it is essentially a silken sheet that resembles a lean-to tent. It has a special area of silk on the underside on which the male deposits inactive sperm. He then fills his bulbs by placing first the tip of one pedipalp and then the other into his deposit. Now ready for action, the male begins his quest for a mate.

Finding a Mate

Females and immature males spend their lives sheltered within a retreat. In many tarantulas, this means a burrow that they seldom leave. They are ambush predators that lie in wait of prey. Some may venture a short distance from the burrow's mouth on occasion, but the tarantula lifestyle is primarily sedentary. For males and females to come together during breeding season, the male must become nomadic and travel some distance in search of a receptive female. This is why at certain times of the year people who would usually never encounter a wild tarantula find them out in the open. These are wandering males that are forced to abandon the safety of cover to find females.

As he looks for the lairs of female tarantulas, the male no longer has a home. He moves incessantly, for the more area he covers the more likely it is that he will come across a receptive female of his species.

The wandering male might be described as frantic or hyperactive as he devotes himself to his reproductive mission. It is thought that the males will be guided by chemical cues in the form of pheromones contained in the silk of the female's retreat to guide them. With any luck, he will avoid predators and other dangers and, with even more good fortune, find a female that will respond to his courtship advances.

A male Gooty Sapphire Ornamental sits safely in his shark tank with the female outside. Once the pair is accustomed to each other, the male will be released for mating.

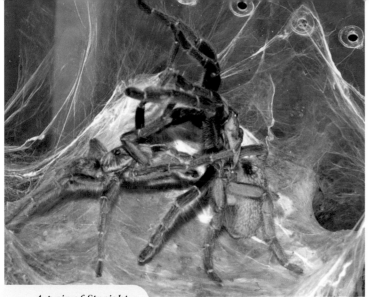

A pair of Straight-Horned Baboon Tarantulas mating.

Courtship

When a mature male tarantula and a mature female tarantula encounter each other, there are two possible scenarios. One is that the female will have little interest in the male except as a potential meal. The other is that the female will be ready to mate. In that case, the male will entice her to leave her shelter by signaling his approach with a series of vibrations caused by the drumming of his appendages and twitching of his body. The courtship dance of tarantulas is not as elaborate as it is in some true spiders, but it is nevertheless a wondrous thing to witness. In many species, the exchange of drumming displays repeats for quite some time, with the male becoming frenetic as his legs thump the ground in a flurry of drum rolls.

Upon closer approach, he may touch her with his forelegs and even tap on her. When the female recognizes the male as a suitor rather than predator or prey, she may respond with her own taps. For the courtship to result in mating the female must have her natural predatory instincts pacified, making her peaceful and receptive; the male must become convinced that he will not be attacked.

A willing female will become passive or may approach the male slowly. She will raise the front of her body and extend her fangs not with aggression, but rather to facilitate copulation. The forelegs of the pair may become entwined as the male and female face each other, and with gentle taps and strokes the two lift their bodies together. In the species where males have tibial hooks, the male engages these hooks with the female's fangs and the two rear up on their hind legs with their undersides off the ground.

As the pair rises together the male will usually reach under the female with his pedipalps and gently brush her opisthosoma. If she continues to consent to his mating desire, he will unfurl the sperm-filled embolus of one pedipalp and quickly insert it into her epigynum. After discharging its contents, he may try a second insertion with his other pedipalp.

Once mating is complete the male holds the female away as he disengages and prepares for a hasty escape. The female often gives a bit of a chase to make the male leave her territory. Despite popular belief, most male tarantulas survive courtship and mating and often go on to mate again. If the male can evade life's other hazards, he will continue his nomadic life, construct additional sperm webs and, hopefully, find another female with which to mate. But his days are limited. Within months of mating, most males become weak and cease feeding. They become vulnerable to predators and may encounter an unreceptive female seeking food, not courtship. This is his final season, and it is up to the next generation to carry on his genes.

Egg Development and Egg Laying

The female tarantula holds the male's sperm in receptacles called spermathecae until conditions are favorable for egg laying. It is beneficial for egg sacs to develop when the climate is stable and for them to hatch when food for the offspring is abundant. Although tarantula keepers often refer to mated females as gravid, this is not technically accurate, as that term refers to an organism that contains fertilized eggs. The female tarantula may begin to ovulate or produce eggs prior to mating or

afterward, but the eggs are not fertilized until they are laid. A female that molts after mating becomes infertile, as the spermathecae lining is also shed, and thus she no longer carries sperm.

Prior to egg laying the female withdraws into her retreat with a shroud of fresh silk. To captive breeders this period is fraught with anticipation as we wonder if the female is just molting or will produce an egg sac. After the time to lay her eggs comes, a female produces silk from a special gland and creates a dense mat of this unique webbing. Once this beginning of her cocoon is constructed, she begins depositing eggs. She will lay from a couple of dozen to a couple of thousand eggs, depending on the species and the female's size and age. The eggs are fertilized just prior to emergence, and once all her eggs have been laid she begins to roll them up into the special silk. She continues to add silk as she works the ball of

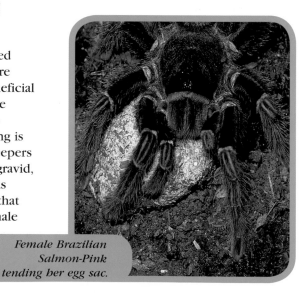

Female Brazilian Salmon-Pink tending her egg sac.

encased eggs into a spherical egg sac. The completed egg sac is held beneath her mouth and rotated periodically using her legs and jaws. This rotation continues during incubation and prevents the eggs from clumping or being affected by the weight of the egg mass above.

The female continues to tend to her egg sac, protecting it and turning it often. She seems to be able to sense its development by the movement of the nymphs inside and will use her jaws to tear a hole so that her early instar babies can emerge and disperse. Incubation time varies with temperature and species, but typically lasts 25 to 90 days. Captive breeders can either leave the egg sac with the female for the duration of incubation and allow spiderlings to emerge as they would in nature or remove the sac for artificial incubation.

Captive Breeding

Once a male has produced a sperm web and charged his pedipalps (or palps in hobby slang), you may introduce him to a female. Often a "shark tank" is employed to protect him until you determine whether the female is receptive. This is a small clear container like a deli-cup that is used to house the male so that he can be placed within the female's enclosure without being in harm's way.

The Expert Knows

Conditioning the Breeding Female

A mated female should be offered as much food as she will accept, with a variety of prey items offered when possible to maximize nutrition. Do not disturb her, and pay extra attention to her environmental conditions. Prior to the initial mating attempt it is wise to rebuild her terrarium with deep substrate and numerous hiding places. She will wait for conditions to be perfect before laying eggs, and ample food, optimal temperature and humidity, and adequate retreats all have a role in stimulating egg sac production.

As each member of the pair becomes aware of each other's presence, they may signal their readiness with a series of taps. The female may move out of her retreat to investigate. By sensing each other through the vibrations of their bodies, as well as detecting chemical cues, they realize that the other is a potential mate and not a meal. Once the two appear to be interested in each other, the lid of the shark tank can be removed to allow the male to move about the terrarium. Many keepers stay at the ready, armed with a couple of spatulas or paintbrushes to use as shields to separate the pair should their interaction become aggressive.

If mating is successful, it may be repeated several times over the course of days or weeks, with males removed during the interim to rest and construct subsequent sperm webs. Repeated mating attempts will increase the chance that viable sperm were transferred to the female.

Seasonal Cycling

In nature, tarantulas may mate at a certain time of the year and then produce egg sacs during a different season. For example, mating may take place during the fall, with the inactive sperm being held in the female's spermathecae until favorable conditions in the spring, when she produces the egg sac. In captivity, some species of tarantulas will produce their egg sacs soon after mating, and this is common in many tropical species. Those that are native to areas where there is significant seasonal fluctuation in weather may require the stimulus of altering their temperature or humidity.

Ornamental tarantulas serve as a good example of a tarantula group naturally from an area with well-defined seasons. They inhabit the Indian subcontinent where weather is affected by the monsoon, resulting in dramatic wet and dry seasons. Keepers who employ seasonal variations—usually by slightly cooling the female after mating—meet the greatest success in breeding ornamental tarantulas.

Manipulating the temperature of the female's enclosure often results in egg

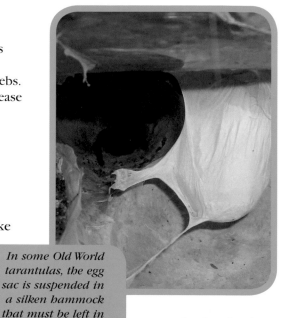

In some Old World tarantulas, the egg sac is suspended in a silken hammock that must be left in the cage to incubate.

sac production for the ornamentals and many other species. Increasing or decreasing moisture and humidity and even photoperiod (light cycle) also may stimulate a female to lay her eggs. To use the ornamental tarantula example, after a female has been mated and has been kept warm (76° to 80°F [24° to 27°C]) and offered plenty of food for a month or so, the keeper will gradually cool her enclosure to about 66° to 68°F (19° to 20°C) for 30 to 60 days. This drop in temperature may not seem like much, but it is all that is necessary to simulate a change in season. If the keeper also decreases moisture and humidity during this time, following that with warming of the enclosure and misting it every day or every other day will replicate a wet and warm season that may trigger egg sac production.

The successful tarantula breeder learns as much as possible about the natural habitat of each species he or she intends to breed so that appropriate cyclical changes can be used to maximize breeding success.

Caring for Egg Sacs

Only a small percentage of pairings will result in a successful mating; that is, a good insertion of the male's palp. Of these matings, only a fraction will result in an egg sac. It is important that the prospective breeder—especially one involved in a breeding loan partnership—is aware that failure is much more common than success. But there are plenty of triumphs. One day you may notice that the female is remaining constantly hidden and may be enveloping herself in a retreat. Very often the shelter becomes enveloped with silk as the female prepares to produce an egg sac. It may be difficult to observe her at all. But once you discover an egg sac, you must make a decision about whether you will leave it to hatch on its own or will incubate it artificially.

Incubation in the Terrarium

If conditions are good within the terrarium (and it is likely they are if a female was willing to produce an egg sac), chances are the sac can be left with the female until 2nd instars emerge. The female will tend to her sac, rotating it with her forelegs, palps, and chelicerae to ensure that the eggs do not clump and become crushed by the weight of the egg mass above. For the novice tarantula breeder, leaving the egg sac with the female for the

When incubating tarantula egg sacs artificially, most breeders tear a small hole in the sac so that they can see when the eggs inside have hatched.

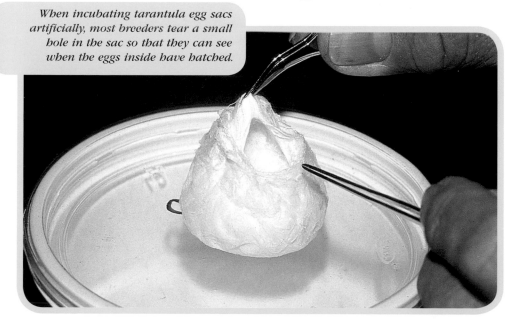

duration of incubation is advised. (Note that some tarantulas—especially African species—produce hammock-style egg sacs that must be left in the cage.) The added benefit of artificial incubation is that upon hatching the spiderlings are contained in a small container instead of being able to disperse in a larger enclosure that may have numerous places to hide.

Artificial Incubation

There are dangers to leaving the sac with the female. If she is disturbed she may damage or even eat the egg sac. Unnoticed prey left in the cage or pest flies may put the egg sac at risk. Mold and fungus are other hazards. Many keepers choose to minimize the threat of losing the egg sac by incubating it artificially for the second half of the incubation period. The egg sac is left with the female for a few weeks or more because it needs to be rotated frequently, and that can be difficult by artificial means. After the female has

The Mechanical Mom

An automated egg sac rotator known in the hobby as a mechanical mom was popularized years ago by the authors of an early tarantula book. This device allows for early egg sac removal or successful incubation of an egg sac that has been abandoned by a female. An Internet search will yield instructions for building your own.

done the hard work of early incubation, the sac is then carefully taken from her using long forceps to gently grasp the sac while she is softly pushed back from it with a second tool like a spatula.

Incubator Cup

An incubator cup protects the egg sac from pests while providing a microenvironment conducive to successful hatching. The basic construction is a cereal bowl-sized food storage container with damp vermiculite on the bottom and a fabric hammock that suspends the egg sac above the substrate. The egg sac must never be placed in direct contact with moisture. The container may have a few tiny holes for ventilation, but you must ensure that even the tiniest of flies cannot enter and that beneficial humidity does not escape.

Vermiculite is an excellent sterile incubation medium and should be moistened just to the point that it clumps before you fill the container one third of the way with it. You can make the fabric hammock out of cheesecloth, panty hose, or similar fabric or even a paper towel. Stretch the hammock across the top of the container and affix it on the outside with a rubber band or tape so that when you place the egg sac in its center the fabric will have a shallow depression but will not come into contact with the damp substrate below. Place the egg sac in the center of the hammock and secure the lid. Keep the incubator cup in a dark and warm location. Once or twice a day,

Eggs and freshly hatched spiderlings of the Common Pink-Toe.

you can gently swirl the cup in the palm of your hand to cause the egg sac to gently roll on the fabric and become rotated.

Incubation Time

The keeper's next task is to determine the time it might take for the eggs to develop. A mother tarantula senses when her nymphs are ready to emerge and tears an opening into the silk egg sac to allow an exit. The keeper will need to fill this role when artificially incubating the sac. Many keepers will cut a slit into the sac and inspect it periodically. Once there are 1st instar young, dump the nymphs directly onto the hammock and discard the empty egg sac. This allows you to spread the nymphs out by gentle use of a small paintbrush, and you can remove any infertile eggs or dead nymphs to prevent mold, fungus, and pests from contaminating the live offspring.

When the 1st instar nymphs begin to darken and approach the molt into 2nd instars, some keepers place a flat piece of cork bark on the damp vermiculite, spill the babies onto the surface of the cork, and discard the hammock. This moves them closer to the moisture, which along with the many contours of the cork bark assists in the molting process. Once the 2nd instar molt is complete and the spiderlings have had several days to harden, you can separate them into individual containers and offer food. Complete instructions for raising the spiderlings can be found in Chapter 2.

Resources

Tarantula Clubs and Societies

American Tarantula Society (ATS)
PO Box 460942
Papillion, NE 68046
www.atshq.org

The British Tarantula Society (BTS)
Angela Hale, Secretary
3 Shepham Lane
Polegate
East Sussex BN26 6LZ
England
E-mail: angehale@thebts.co.uk
www.thebts.co.uk

Tarantula Internet Forums

Arachnoboards
www.arachnoboards.com

ATS Discussion Board
atshq.org/forum/index.php

BTS Forum
www.thebts.co.uk/forums/index.php

Other Online Resources

Arachnoculture E-Zine
 www.exoticfauna.com/arachnoculture.
html

A Key to the Pronunciation and Meaning
of Scientific Names of Popular Species
Part I: Pronunciation: http://atshq.org/
articles/beechwp1.html
Part II: Meaning: http://atshq.org/
articles/beechwp2.html

The Tarantula Bibliography
www.tarantulabibliography.net

The Tarantula's Burrow
arachnophiliac.info/burrow/home.htm

Sexing Tarantulas

Microscopic examination of exuvia
(molts) (the author's free tarantula
sexing service)
www.exoticfauna.com/tarantula_sexing.
html

For more information on the epiandrous
fusillae method of tarantula sexing see
http://www.birdspiders.com/faq_sex.
php

Tarantula Images

Birdspiders
www.birdspiders.com/gallery/index.php

Books

Hellweg, Michael R. *Raising Live Foods*.
TFH Publications, 2009
Purser, Philip. *Natural Terrariums*. TFH
    Publications, 2007

Index

Boldfaced numbers indicate illustrations.

Tarantulas

111

Index

Dedication

For my mother, Judith, who both tolerated and encouraged my boyhood passion for creepy crawlies and the house full of spiders and snakes that resulted from it. Some forty years later, the passion (and support) continues.

With thanks to two great tarantula men: Ralph Henning, of Joliet, Illinois, turned this reptile guy into an arachnid guy too. He is one of the American pioneers of tarantula keeping and breeding and I hope this mention will make more people aware of that. Andrew M. Smith, the eminent British arachnohistorian, inspired me with his incredible books long before I met him, and has encouraged me in the years I have been privileged to call him a close friend. Cheers to both.

Acknowledgements

Many heartfelt thanks to my sister Lisa Uidl who has always been willing to give my writings a critical read. I am also grateful to my editor Tom Mazorlig and his Animal Planet and TFH Publications teams. A number of fellow arachnid enthusiasts have inspired and supported me over a lifetime of tarantula keeping and they are far too numerous to list here, but I would like to make special mention of a few pioneers of North American tarantulaculture—Rick C. West, Allan McKee, and Stanley Schultz—and some of my fellow tarantula breeders including William Korinek, Kelly Swift, Frank Somma, Eric Reynolds, and Alex Orleans. Cheers also to the entire Committee of the British Tarantula Society, where I am privileged to serve as North American Representative.

Tarantulas

About the Author

Michael Andreas Jacobi is general manager at a wholesale pet company and has kept and bred tarantulas, reptiles, and other terrarium pets for more than 35 years. He operates the tarantulas.com website, is the North American Representative of the British Tarantula Society, and has lectured at ArachnoCon and both American and British Tarantula Society conferences. He is the creator of *ARACHNOCULTURE* magazine and e-zine and of the online resource The Tarantula Bibliography. Originally from the Chicago area, Michael now lives north of Seattle, Washington, with his dog Taylor. Visit him at ExoticFauna.com

Photo Credits

2happy (from Shutterstock): 61; Art-man (from Shutterstock.com): 26; R.D. Bartlett: 41, 89; Creatista (from Shutterstock.com): 90 (bottom); Cyrrpit (from Shutterstock.com): 33 (top); Five Spots (from Shutterstock.com): 7; Formiktopus (from Shutterstock.com): 12, 79; James E. Gerholdt: 90 (top), 95; Iliuta Goean (from Shutterstock.com): back cover (top); Katherine Haluska (from Shutterstock.com): 80 (bottom left); Ifong (from Shutterstock.com): 11; Eric Isselée (from Shutterstock.com): 3, 39; Michael Andreas Jacobi: 6, 8, 15 (top), 23, 27, 29, 31, 32, 33 (bottom), 37, 51, 52, 53, 54, 56, 58, 65, 72, 81 (top), 83, 85, 87 (top, bottom right), 92, 93 (all), 96, 98, 100, 101, 104, back cover (center top and center bottom); Natalie Jean (from Shutterstock.com): 13, 16; Cathy Keifer (from Shutterstock.com): 4, 50 (all), 57, 66, 84; Rich Lindie (from Shutterstock.com): 48; Erik Loza: 34; Luka TDB (from Shutterstock.com): 44; maxstockphoto (from Shutterstock.com): 74; G. and C. Merker: 15, 70, 80; Gerald L. Moore: 14, 17, 20, 86, 105, 107; Peter Pech (from Shutterstock.com): 94; Audrey Snider-Bell (from Shutterstock.com): front cover, 10, 76, 87 (bottom left), 88, 89 (top), 91; K. H. Switak: 69, 102; withGod (from Shutterstock.com): 64; Paul S. Wolf (from Shutterstock.com): 80 (bottom right)